DREAMERS WHO LEAD

Dreamers Who Lead

HECTOR A. IBARRA

Praise for Dreamers Who Lead: A Leadership Memoir.

"From personal experience, Hector Ibarra shows that achieving one's management dream takes more than diligence, luck, and persistence. It also requires soft skills in motivating others, connecting up and down an organizational hierarchy, and being sensitive to the economic demands of a company's constituents."
— *Bruce Jacobs, Retired CEO, Grede Foundries*

Dreamers Who Lead: A Leadership Memoir
By Héctor A. Ibarra

Copyright © 2026 The Road of a Dreamer, LLC

All rights reserved. No part of this book may be reproduced, stored in a retrieval system, or transmitted in any form or by any means, electronic, mechanical, photocopying, recording, or otherwise, without the prior written permission of the author, except in the case of brief quotations used in critical articles or reviews.

This is a work of nonfiction based on the author's personal memories and life experiences. Some names and identifying details have been changed to respect the privacy of individuals.

First Edition, 2026

ISBN: 979-8-9940261-5-1

Cover design and interior formatting by Héctor Ibarra

in collaboration with ChatGPT by OpenAI

Printed in the United States of America

Published by The Road of a Dreamer LLC – www.theroadofadreamer.com

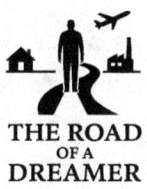

Disclaimer

This book is based on the author's personal experiences, reflections, and opinions throughout his career. Certain names, roles, and identifying details have been changed or omitted to protect the privacy of individuals. Any resemblance to actual persons, living or dead, is coincidental.

References to companies or organizations are included only as part of the author's professional journey and are not intended to represent, describe, or evaluate those companies in their entirety. The lessons and opinions expressed in this book are solely those of the author and do not reflect the official policies or positions of any employer, past or present.

The author has made every effort to ensure the accuracy of the information shared in this book. However, this book is not intended as professional, legal, or business advice. Readers are encouraged to apply their own judgment and discretion in interpreting the lessons shared.

This book is intended for educational and inspirational purposes only.

"This book should be read as a personal narrative and leadership reflection, not as a representation of any specific person, company, or event."

DEDICATION

To every dreamer who chose to lead— not because it was easy, but because it mattered.

To the workers who show up early, the managers who stay late, and the leaders who carry the weight of both.

To those who build not just products and processes, but trust, purpose, and possibility.

To the readers of The Road of a Dreamer who encouraged me to write about leadership, thank you. Your support gave this book purpose.

To my wife Patricia, my daughter Anna, and to all my family and friends— thank you for standing by me, for believing in The Road of a Dreamer, and for encouraging me to keep writing.

To every young engineer, may this book offer guidance, encouragement,
and a few hard-earned lessons to smooth your path.

To Patricio Gil, and Bruce Jacobs —not only for contributing their words to this book, but for generously sharing their knowledge, time, and exchange of ideas throughout this journey.

And to every experienced manager, may it serve as a tool to grow the next generation of leaders.

This book is for you.

Prologue
Patricio Gil
President & CEO, MAPPSA / Savelli North America

Leadership is a highly interesting topic and, moreover, a critical one for the different entities that make up a society to evolve in the direction desired by those involved. It is not possible to improvise and believe that we will reach a desired final state.

There are many types of leadership described in business literature, and it is not the purpose of this book to delve deeply into them; ultimately, there are no better or worse leadership styles. What matters is that the leader and their style are aligned with the environment, with their team, with the resources available, and with the challenges they face.

Based on my personal experience in the business world, in a globalized and highly competitive environment such as the automotive industry, I have had—and continue to have—many learnings throughout my more than forty years of active professional career.

I began in the foundry industry, like most recent graduates, as an engineer with no personnel reporting to me and with assigned tasks that I had to carry out on my own. Gradually, I grew within the organization until becoming plant manager and later general manager at the age of 34. From that point on, I held general manager positions until the age of 57, when I decided to leave corporate life as an employee to venture into my own business manufacturing precision components for the industry.

At the same time, I always maintained active participation in professional organizations, eventually serving as president of two very important foundry organizations: the Ductile Iron Society, based in Cleveland, and the American Foundry Society, the largest foundry organization in the world, headquartered in Chicago with more than 8,000 members—being to this day the only president of that organization who is not a citizen of the United States.

Throughout this journey, I have learned many things about leadership. The first is that the higher you are, the lonelier you become. This means you are more visible within the organization and must be willing to assume the risks that come with that visibility.

Publicly assuming responsibility for results before your team and stakeholders is a fundamental characteristic of a leader. A leader may delegate authority, but must never delegate responsibility to external parties.

Therefore, everything must start with a vision. The leader must be convinced of the need and importance of moving the organization from its current state to a desired future state. This must be broken down into strategies, objectives, intermediate stages, resources, indicators, and goals. If this process is not clear, it is very difficult to reach the desired future state.

On the other hand, if the plan is properly communicated, tasks, resources, and responsibilities are distributed, and consistent follow-up is provided, progress will surely be made in the desired direction.

The leader must be concerned with building a work team that is multi-skilled. They must define the skills and knowledge that the team, as a whole, should possess and ensure that team members complement one another. It is not about everyone knowing everything, but about enriching the team through the diversity of its members.

Once the desired scenario and the way forward have been defined, follow-up actions must be implemented. At this point, it is important not to fall into the mistake of defining an excessive number of indicators without order or priority.

A very common bad habit that must be avoided is filling the day with meetings. Teamwork does not consist of deciding everything collectively, but rather of sharing a common objective and executing with individual responsibility.

The leader must not lose sight of who their main customers are: those who consume their products and the shareholders who expect a return on their investment.

Another lesson from the globalized world is the richness of multiculturalism. Practices can be standardized, but styles cannot.

It is difficult to capture so many years of learning in just a few words, but I can summarize by saying that a leader must have vision, share it, act with consistency, assume consequences, recognize strengths and weaknesses, build strong teams, and always be responsible for the direction of the organization they lead.

I thank Héctor for the distinction of inviting me to participate in this book. I have witnessed his professional growth, the passion he brings to what he does, and now the enormous challenge of writing books. I wish him great success and am confident that his experiences will help enrich the journey of many leaders. Congratulations!

— **Patricio Gil**

Author's Comments

After sharing my life's journey in The Road of a Dreamer, many readers asked what came next, what lessons had I learned, and how had I applied them along the way. This book is that answer.

Dreamers Who Lead is a continuation of the path I've traveled, but now with a focus on leadership, the hard truths, the personal stories, the principles that guided me, and the mistakes that shaped me. It is not a manual, but a collection of reflections from a dreamer who learned to lead, sometimes the hard way.

My hope is that these stories will resonate with you—whether you're on the shop floor, in the boardroom, or somewhere in between. If The Road of a Dreamer helped you believe in your journey, then may this book help you lead others through theirs.

Because at the end of the day, it's not just about dreaming big, it's about leading with purpose to turn those dreams into reality.

Table of Contents

Part I: The Foundations of Effective Leadership

- Chapter 1. Safety Is Number One... or Is It?
- Chapter 2. Quality and the Result of Following Procedures
- Chapter 3. Productivity Is the Result, Not the Goal
- Chapter 4. Housekeeping and First Impressions
- Chapter 5. Thinking Outside the Box

Part II: People, Power, and Practice

- Chapter 6. Teamwork: Easier Said Than Done
- Chapter 7. Maintenance: From Superheroes to Ghosts
- Chapter 8. The Hardest and Easiest Thing to Do—Discipline
- Chapter 9. Respect at All Levels
- Chapter 10. We Always Punish the Best Employees: How to Protect and Empower Top Talent
- Chapter 11. Not Making a Decision Is Also a Decision
- Chapter 12. Estimating and Budgeting: The Numbers Behind Leadership Decisions
- Chapter 13. The Power of Communication and Feedback (as a Growth Tool)

Part III: Personal Growth in Professional Spaces

- Chapter 14. Promote Yourself—There's Nothing Wrong with That
- Chapter 15. Sales Is Not About Selling—It's About Solving a Problem
- Chapter 16. You Can't Lead Well on an Empty Tank
- Chapter 17. It's Only Business, Not Personal

- Chapter 18. Partnering with Human Resources — Leading People, Not Just Processes
- Chapter 19. Industrial and Process Engineering: Designing Systems for People and Performance.
- Chapter 20. New Technologies to Simplify and Eliminate

Part IV: Leading with Wisdom and Integrity

- Chapter 21. Traps and Mistakes Leaders Can Commit
- Chapter 22. Leading Through Change and Conflict
- Chapter 23. Mentoring and Developing Others
- Chapter 24. The Leader's Horizon: Balancing Today and Tomorrow
- Chapter 25. Resilience and Well-Being: Balancing Leadership and Life

Part V: The Future of Leadership

- Chapter 26. Leading in Crisis: Calm in the Storm
- Chapter 27. Diversity and Global Leadership
- Chapter 28. Sustainability and Responsibility in Leadership
- Chapter 29. Final Words from a Dreamer Who Leads

Chapter 1. Safety Is Number One... or Is It?

"Safety fails the moment leaders assume everything is fine."

Throughout my years working across different companies and industries, there has been one constant: everyone claims that safety is their number one priority. You hear it everywhere—slogans like "Nothing is so important that it can't be done safely." They sound great. But in practice, I've learned the biggest threat to safety isn't just faulty equipment or lack of training, it's overconfidence.

People often think they know a process so well that nothing could ever go wrong. They believe they're too smart, too experienced, or too quick for accidents to happen. But let's be honest, most people don't like following rules unless they absolutely have to.

If you're reading this thinking, "I always follow the rules," I'd challenge you to reflect: have you ever gone just a little over the speed limit? Or partied a bit too hard but still decided to drive home? Most of us bend the rules occasionally because we trust ourselves to handle the risk. That same mentality exists in the workplace.

I've seen operators skip wearing safety glasses or earplugs because "nothing ever happens." I've seen managers walk through production floors without PPE because "they're not the ones doing the work." **But leadership isn't about exceptions; it's about example. When management cuts corners, it signals to everyone else that safety is optional.**

And that's a dangerous message.

The Human Cost of Overconfidence

I've witnessed several serious accidents in my career. Thankfully, none resulted in fatalities, but they all had something in common: they were 100% preventable.

One of my earliest lessons came while I was still at university in Mexico, during an internship at a well-known factory in Saltillo that manufactured cutlery. The process was simple but incredibly risky. A large mechanical press would take sheets of metal and stamp out pieces. The press never stopped. Operators had to manually guide the material into the machine, carefully keeping their hands away.

It was my first week when I saw the ambulance arrive. A night shift operator, probably exhausted or distracted, miscalculated. The press came down on his hand, crushing it completely. That single moment changed his life—and his family's future—forever. Today, such a setup would be illegal. Machines now require two-hand controls, light curtains, or robotic automation to protect operators.

Years later, at another plant, an operator was grinding the inside of a turbo housing. To do it properly, he had to wear a face shield and use a hand grinder with a protective guard. But he removed the guard—it made the job easier. When the grinding disc shattered under pressure, fragments flew out. One piece lodged into his cheek. He needed nine stitches, and the scar never left him. I remember calling his wife to explain what happened. She rushed in, panicked and in tears. That moment stayed with me.

These are stark reminders that safety is not just about compliance is about families, lives, and futures.

A Lesson They Never Forgot

One of the most memorable efforts I've seen came from a passionate safety leader on my team. She wanted to break away from typical PowerPoint training and do something people would never forget.

Her idea was bold. We set up a special meeting room with real photos of workplace injuries. At the center there was a coffin. Inside, a volunteer employee played the role of the deceased. We hired actors: a priest, a mother, and a wife. They wept, cried out, and asked the employees why they didn't protect him—why they didn't look out for each other.

The impact was immediate. Some workers cried; others were visibly shaken. Though everyone knew it wasn't real, it felt real enough to leave a lasting mark. People talked about it for weeks. That safety manager Karina Rodriguez later received recognition in the UK and went on to lead global safety efforts in Brazil.

Why Safety Makes Sense

Safety is not only morally right, but it also makes financial sense. Insurance premiums skyrocket with accidents, and the costs of downtime, investigations, and employee turnover add up. But above all, no number can measure the cost of a broken family or a life-altering injury.

The lesson I've learned is simple: Invest in safety. Live it. Breathe it. Walk the talk. Never walk onto the floor without the proper PPE. If you don't think safety is important, your team won't either.

And most importantly—remember this: You may be the one who must explain to someone's family why their loved one isn't coming home. That's a conversation no leader ever wants to have.

Beyond Checklists: Building a Safety Culture

As leaders, we're not just responsible for results. We're responsible for people—their lives, their futures, and their families. Let's never forget that.

Safety isn't achieved through slogans or posters on the wall. It becomes real when it's part of the culture. In some of our facilities, we went over 1,000 days without a single accident. That kind of success doesn't happen by chance. It takes everyone: following guidelines, reporting issues early, and trusting that leadership will respond. The key is creating an environment where people feel safe to speak up—and know they'll be heard.

These tragic stories are stark reminders of why training isn't just a requirement, it's a lifeline. That's why we ensure our teams receive consistent, practical safety training each month.

Training: A Critical Foundation

Communication is a powerful tool in building this culture. In all the companies I've worked for, we maintained a monthly calendar of training topics. These weren't just OSHA-required sessions; they were essential reminders that kept the team aware, engaged, and protected.

Here are some of the required monthly safety topics (in no particular order):

Bloodborne Pathogens: Training employees to stay safe when exposed to blood or other potentially infectious materials.
Hazard Communication: Understanding chemical hazards, proper labeling, Safety Data Sheets (SDS), and employee rights.
Respiratory Protection: Proper use, selection, and maintenance of respirators.
Hearing Conservation: Protecting hearing from noise exposure and understanding long-term damage risks.
Fire Extinguishers: Types, usage, and hands-on practice for different fire scenarios.
Lockout/Tagout: Procedures for isolating energy sources to safely perform maintenance.

Powered Industrial Trucks: Safe operation and inspection of forklifts and similar equipment (required every three years but recommended annually).

Emergency Action Plan: How to react to weather events, fires, or active shooter threats.

Personal Protective Equipment (PPE): Selection, proper use, limitations, maintenance, and disposal.

Slips, Trips, and Falls Prevention: Best practices to avoid common workplace injuries.

Electrical Safety Awareness: Recognizing electrical hazards and appropriate PPE requirements.

Machine Guard Awareness: Identifying guarding hazards and ensuring equipment safety.

Ergonomics and Safe Lifting: Preventing strains and musculoskeletal injuries.

First Aid / CPR: Awareness refreshers and practice if applicable.

Workplace Violence Prevention: Recognition, reporting procedures, and de-escalation techniques.

Hot Work Permit Program: Safe procedures for welding, cutting, or brazing operations.

Confined Space Awareness: Requirements for entrants and attendants per permit programs.

Fall Protection: Proper use of equipment when working at heights.

Environmental Compliance/Spill Prevention: Procedures to minimize environmental risks.

While some of these are mandatory, I always recommend reviewing all topics annually, emphasizing those most critical for your operations and ensuring every new employee is trained from day one.

Leading by Example

Another powerful tool is daily safety conversation. Supervisors should take five minutes each day to talk to their team about safety, listen to concerns, and act on them. These builds trust and ensures issues don't get buried under production pressures.

Perhaps the most powerful act a leader can do is walk the floor with safety as the only purpose. Not to check production, not to correct performance, but to observe: What's out of place? What looks off? What risks are lurking?

These focused walks send a clear message: "I care about this because I care about you." When people see that, they start to care too. That's how real safety is built—not with slogans or inspections, but with trust, consistency, and leaders who lead by example.

Reflection:

Think about your own workplace. When was the last time you *truly* stopped to observe how safety is practiced — not just discussed? What message do your actions send? Do people see you taking shortcuts, or do they see you taking the time to do things right?

Challenge:

1. **Take one day this week** to walk your area or team space with new eyes. Don't look for faults; look for habits. Notice where people have made safety personal — and where it has become routine.
2. **Start one small conversation** about safety that has nothing to do with compliance. Ask someone, *"What would make your job safer or easier?"* Then listen — and act on one idea.

3. **Lead by example.** The next time you see a risk, don't delegate it or document it — address it, fix it, or model the right behavior immediately.

Final Thought:

Safety isn't a rule; it's a reflection of leadership.
The moment people see you care enough to protect them — even in the smallest ways — is the moment they start caring for one another.

Chapter 2. Quality and the Result of Following Procedures
"Quality collapses one shortcut at a time."

One of the main reasons the Quality Department exists is to serve as the guardian of standards—the enforcer of rules. Think of it like the cop on the highway when you're tempted to go 100 miles per hour in a 70-mph zone. You might know the speed limit, but without enforcement, the temptation to cut corners can be too strong to resist.

Everyone says quality is important. Everyone agrees that meeting customer requirements and specifications is crucial—unless it's the end of the month and the pressure is on to hit production numbers. That's when people start to compromise, justify shortcuts, and tell themselves they'll "do it right next time." But that kind of thinking is exactly what gets companies into trouble.

Sometimes the damage is a minor disappointment to customers or a returned product. Other times, it's massive—multi-million-dollar recalls, legal action, and irreparable harm to the brand. All because someone didn't follow the process.

At one of the companies I worked for, the production system was still based on piece rate. That meant the more parts you produced, the more money you earned. On the surface, it sounded great: productivity went up, operators were motivated, and supervisors were happy. But beneath that surface, a dangerous imbalance was growing.

Quality checks were in place. Audits were performed. But when you're running multiple cells with limited supervision, it's hard to keep eyes on everything. Piece rate unintentionally trained people to care more about how fast they worked rather than how well they worked.

Industrial Engineers set the cycle times to allow operators to meet their quotas with some extra room to earn bonuses. Operators quickly learned to beat those rates. But what got left behind? Safety and quality.

When you're rushing to hit a number, you skip steps. Lubricating the dies every cycle turns into every second or third cycle. Visual inspections become less frequent. People start playing with the limits of the process until—inevitably—something fails. And by the time the inspector raises the issue, the damage is done.

I saw what was happening and knew it had to change. I proposed moving away from the piece rate to an hourly wage—one that was fair and competitive. My message to the operators was simple:

"I don't want you to go so fast that you compromise quality. If you're trying to earn 20% more pay, but that leads to 10% scrap, we all lose. I'd rather pay a solid hourly rate and keep scrap below 1%. Why rush, only to waste time, materials, and effort?"

At first, some were skeptical. But as we implemented the new system and partnered with the operators to understand the importance of standard processes, something happened: scrap levels dropped, and the number of good parts stayed consistent. Quality improved. The work became more sustainable. We weren't just making parts—we were building confidence in the process.

Living the Audit

One of my core beliefs about quality systems is this:

You shouldn't prepare for an audit. You should live the audit.

If you have a system that truly works, it means you say what you do—and you do what you say. An audit shouldn't be a performance. It should be a snapshot of your reality.

Some people panic when an auditor shows up. They scramble to clean up files, organize documents, or quickly patch over weak spots. But that's not an improvement; that's an illusion. And illusion doesn't build trust.

If an auditor finds a weakness, that's not a failure. It's a gift. Yes, it might be uncomfortable. It might even hurt. But it's a chance to get better. And if we're serious about quality, that's all that should matter.

When we find an issue, we apply corrective action. Then we go further—transform that into a preventive action and make it part of the system. Cheating on an audit is just cheating yourself, your people, and your company.

Quality Across Cultures

Having worked in different companies across various countries, I've seen firsthand how culture influences quality—not just in outcomes, but in how rules, processes, and discipline are understood and accepted.

In countries like Japan, there's a strong cultural emphasis on order, precision, and respect for the process. People are taught from a young age to follow instructions, contribute to group harmony, and take pride in consistent execution. Quality is not something imposed—it's something ingrained. It's how they live, not just how they work.

Germany is similar in that sense. Methodical thinking, structured systems, and a commitment to rules are part of the national character. When a process is designed, it's meant to be followed. People respect the logic behind it.

But in North America—both in the U.S. and Mexico—the cultural dynamic is different. People here often question the rules. They challenge authority, experiment with alternatives, and feel a strong sense of ownership over their work. It's part of what drives innovation, creativity, and problem-solving—but it also introduces risk, especially in manufacturing.

Here's the conflict:

The operators are the ones doing the job. They often do know better than anyone what works and what doesn't. But without consistency, even the best insights get lost in the noise.

If every person runs the process their way, how do we know which method produces quality? When chaos becomes the norm, it's impossible to identify what caused success—or failure. That's the challenge many companies face.

The solution isn't rigid standardization that strips away all individuality. It's engineered discipline—designing workstations, procedures, and systems that provide room for creativity within a controlled structure. You want just enough flexibility for input, but not so much that ten people do the same job ten different ways.

That's what quality leadership looks like in a multicultural, multi-plant, global organization:

Respect the culture. Honor the insight. Build the system. Enforce the standard.
Quality is not just a department. It's a mindset. It's leadership in action.

Essential Quality Tools — and How to Use Them Wisely

While cultural mindset shapes how we approach quality, having the right tools empowers leaders to translate those mindsets into action.

Core Problem-Solving and Process Tools

- **Cause and Effect Diagram (Fishbone or Ishikawa Diagram):** Identifies root causes of problems, visualizing potential causes under categories (man, machine, method, material, measurements, environment).
- **Pareto Chart:** Identifies the most significant factors based on the 80/20 principle to prioritize improvement efforts.
- **Control Chart:** Monitors process variation over time to determine process stability and identify trends.
- **Flowchart:** Visualizes process steps and decision points, useful for understanding and improving workflows.
- **Histogram:** Displays frequency distributions and variation patterns for easy analysis.

Measurement and Data Analysis Tools

- **Scatter Diagram:** Visualizes correlations between variables to assess relationships (strong, weak, positive, negative).
- **Check Sheets:** Simple forms for collecting and analyzing data systematically.
- **Process Capability Analysis (Cp, Cpk, Pp, Ppk):** Determines process ability to produce within specification.
- **Gage R&R:** Evaluates measurement system variation.
- **Regression Analysis:** Models and predict relationships between variables for continuous improvement.

Risk and System Improvement Tools

- **Failure Mode and Effects Analysis (FMEA):** Identifies potential failure modes and prioritizes corrective actions.
- **Design of Experiments (DOE):** Guides structured experimentation for process optimization.
- **Statistical Process Control (SPC):** Uses control charts and statistical analysis to maintain process stability.
- **Root Cause Analysis (RCA):** Includes 5 Whys, Fishbone Diagrams, and Fault Tree Analysis for systematic problem solving.
- **Affinity Diagram:** Organizes large amounts of data into logical groupings for clarity.

"If you're new to these, start small. Master Pareto and Root Cause Analysis first — they'll change how you see problems. Once you build that discipline, the rest come naturally."

These tools are the foundation of every quality system—but tools alone don't build excellence. What makes the difference is how leaders use them.

Over time, the real improvement doesn't come from the charts or the data; it comes from how they change the way you think. Quality isn't about reacting to defects; it's about building habits that prevent them from ever happening.

Reader Reflection

A leader doesn't just enforce procedures, they explain why those procedures matter. A leader doesn't chase numbers—they pursue standards. When quality becomes everyone's responsibility, it becomes part of the culture.

If you want a strong operation, don't just ask for results. Ask for consistency. Ask for integrity. Build a system where people take pride in doing it right the first time, every time—not just when someone is watching.

Ask yourself:

- Does your team see quality as inspection or as pride in craftsmanship?
- Am I rewarding shortcuts or reinforcing discipline?

Challenge:

This week, perform an unannounced "quality walk" through your workplace. Observe, listen, and ask questions. Look for small improvements you can make immediately—and involve your team in creating them.

Chapter 3. Productivity Is the Result, Not the Goal
"Productivity rises when processes support people—not when people are pushed harder."

Once quality becomes habit, productivity follows naturally.

Every business ultimately exists to deliver a product or a service—so it's no surprise that productivity often becomes the central focus. Over time, we've developed countless tools and metrics to track how much we produce, how fast, and how efficiently. The pressure to deliver more in less time is relentless.

But when this pressure dominates, as we've explored in earlier chapters, it can quietly push aside critical priorities like safety and quality. The mindset becomes: Just get the product out the door—whatever it takes. And that's where things start to go wrong.

My approach has always been different. I believe productivity is not the goal, it's the outcome. When we do everything right, productivity comes naturally. The real focus should be on creating the conditions that make that result inevitable.

If:

Procedures are clear and followed,
People are properly trained,
The equipment is well-maintained,
Tools and materials are available when needed,
…then everything works like the gears of a fine watch. Smooth. Precise. Reliable.

But when we obsess over the result—output—we start making dangerous trade-offs:

Skip maintenance to avoid downtime.
Delay training because we're "too busy."
Ignore procedure development to save time.

And all of these shortcut's lead to the exact outcome we were trying to avoid: missed deadlines, poor quality, unsafe conditions, and unhappy customers.

So, what's the solution?

Focus on the inputs.

As a leader in operations, your job is not to chase results, it's to create the environment that produces them. Build a culture and a team that understands this mindset. Challenge your team to ask, "What's standing in the way of doing things right?" and dig deep to uncover the true root causes.

Many times, the bottleneck isn't a machine, it's the lack of attention it gets. It's not an operator, it's the absence of tools, training, or motivation.

When people understand why their work matters and have the resources to do it well, their mindset shifts. They're no longer just running parts or checking boxes—they're contributing to something that works. Something that wins.

A Real-World Lesson on Misaligned Incentives

Some of the most common challenges I've encountered during turnaround assignments didn't originate on the production floor—they started in the office, at the top.

In one facility I was asked to turn around, I quickly discovered a pattern: the plant manager's bonus was directly tied to the number of units shipped and overall sales generated. At first glance, that seems reasonable—you reward performance, right?

But here's the problem: when upper management is financially incentivized solely by output, it opens the door to shortcuts. And that's exactly what happened.

To meet targets and maximize bonuses, they began skipping essential tasks, postponing maintenance, reducing training hours, and ignoring procedural updates. For a while, the numbers looked great. They shipped more, reported fewer expenses, and celebrated "efficiency."

But it was an illusion.

Eventually, the consequences started catching up. Machines break down more often. Quality complaints increased. Safety incidents began to rise. And just when things began to fall apart, those same leaders moved, retired, transferred, or took jobs at other companies—leaving someone else to clean up the mess.

That someone was me.

What I found wasn't a broken team, it was a broken system. People weren't lazy or incompetent. They had simply been conditioned to prioritize the wrong things because the system rewarded them for doing so.

Was it unethical? In my opinion, yes.

But was it predictable based on how the bonus plan was structured? Also, yes.

That experience taught me a valuable lesson: you get what you measure—and what you reward.

If you reward only production, you'll get it—at the cost of everything else. But if you build a compensation model that includes performance in safety, quality, maintenance, and training, you create a culture that values long-term success over short-term wins.

Incentives shape behavior. As leaders, it's our job to shape them wisely.

Essential Productivity Tools for Leaders

Some tools that will help a production leader to be more efficient are the following. As with previous chapters, these are listed for awareness, and further investigation should be conducted to integrate them effectively:

Manufacturing Execution Systems (MES). Monitors production status, downtime, scrap, cycle times. Examples: Ignition, Plex, ShopVue, Siemens Opcenter.

OEE Monitoring Systems. Calculates Overall Equipment Efficiency to identify losses in availability, performance, and quality. Examples: Vorne XL, OEE Coach, FactoryWiz.

Digital Dashboards and BI Tools. Consolidate production KPIs, trends, and historical analysis for strategic decisions. Examples: Power BI, Tableau, Qlik Sense.

SCADA Systems (Supervisory Control and Data Acquisition). Monitor and control automated process operations in real time.

Time and Motion Study Tools. Analyze task times for optimization. Examples: Timer Pro, stopwatch tools.

Lean Manufacturing Tools. Value Stream Mapping (VSM), 5S audits, standard work creation and audits, SMED (Single Minute Exchange of Die) for quick changeovers.

Six Sigma Tools. DMAIC methodology for structured problem-solving. Statistical tools (Minitab for data analysis), control charts, process capability analysis.

Kaizen Event Frameworks. Structured continuous improvement workshops to engage teams in rapid productivity improvements.

Digital Work Instructions. Standardized, easy-to-update digital instructions reduce variability. Examples: Dozuki, SwipeGuide.

Task Management and Workflow Tools. Project and task tracking within improvement teams. Examples: Trello, Asana.

Simulation Software. Model and optimize production lines before implementation. Examples: Arena, Simul8, FlexSim.

Aligning the Team Around the Right Focus

There are several steps leaders can take to ensure the team is focused on the right things. One of the most important is alignment—making sure everyone shares the same vision, mission, and values. These aren't just corporate buzzwords; they're the foundation that holds everything together. When these elements are unclear or inconsistent, the entire operation begins to drift.

Let's start with vision and mission.

Vision answers the question: Where are we going? It should paint a compelling picture of the future—something your team wants to help build. It must be clear, inspiring, and memorable.

Mission explains what we do, for whom, and why it matters. A good mission connects people to purpose. When employees know how their work contributes to something meaningful, their engagement—and performance—naturally improve.

Then come the values, the core behaviors that guide how we work every day:

Respect: Treating everyone fairly and with dignity.

Accountability: Taking ownership of our responsibilities.

Integrity: Doing the right thing, even when no one is watching.

Excellence: Striving for continuous improvement.

Teamwork: Supporting each other and collaborating toward shared goals.

But having values on paper isn't enough, they must be lived. That means recognizing when someone models them well, and just as importantly, addressing when they're not being upheld. As a leader, you set the tone by living those values every day.

When your team is aligned around a common vision, mission, and set of values, you create clarity. Clarity leads to consistency. And consistency leads to results.

That's why productivity is not something you chase, it's something you earn. When you do the right things the right way, productivity follows.

Just like I've learned in life and leadership, true success never comes from shortcuts—it comes from doing things right, every time.

And that's the kind of leadership that transforms not just teams—but entire organizations.

Because true dreamers don't just chase results—they build legacies

Chapter 4. Housekeeping and First Impressions

"If you want to know how a plant runs, look at the areas no one shows on the tour."

To begin developing a strong team, the first step is always good housekeeping. And no—this isn't just about making the workplace look nicer (although that alone should be a motivator). It's about instilling discipline, which is the foundation for building a high-performing and reliable organization.

In several companies I've worked with, it was considered "normal" for the workplace to be dirty or poorly lit. The justification? "Our process is too messy to keep clean." In iron foundries—whether gray or ductile—we used green sand to hold molten metal and shape castings. It's a messy process, especially when cores are involved. In forging facilities, scaling from hot billets and the use of graphite lubricants can make things even more challenging.

But here's the truth: cleanliness is always possible—and it always matters.

A clean environment isn't just about aesthetics. It directly impacts safety, quality, and productivity. More importantly, it sets the tone. A clean workplace signals that we care about our process, our product, and—most importantly—our people.

To illustrate this point, I often show teams two photos. One is a pristine, well-lit hospital room. The other is a dark, filthy, cluttered space with trash and stains. Then I ask: Which room would you prefer to have surgery in?

The answer is always the same—the clean room. When I ask why, people say it feels safer—that it gives the impression of having competent doctors, strong procedures, and the right conditions for success.

Then I ask: But what if both rooms had the same doctors and procedures?

That's when the message sinks in.

Perception matters. When customers or executives visit a plant for the first time, what do they see? If the workplace is chaotic and dirty, they will question whether the team has discipline or the ability to follow procedures. They may begin to doubt whether their products—or trust—are in the right hands.

If we can't cover the basics, how can we expect others to believe we'll handle the complex?

As leaders, we must start with the fundamentals. Discipline begins with housekeeping. A clean, organized environment creates pride, accountability, and trust. Start small—clean one area, organizing one zone, eliminate one excuse. The results will compound.

Tools to Enhance Housekeeping and Discipline

To help you accomplish these tasks, here are some tools that, if properly applied, will enhance your housekeeping efforts and, more importantly, build the organization and discipline that lead your company to higher results.

Visual Management Tools

Shadow Boards and Tool Organizers. Outline spaces for tools to ensure everything is returned to its place, avoiding wasted time searching. Provides quick visual confirmation of missing tools.
Floor Markings and Labels. Color-coded tape or paint to define walkways, storage areas, and safety zones. Labels for shelves, racks, and bins maintain organization.
Signage and Visual Standards. Standardize signs for cleaning schedules, PPE requirements, and equipment status.

Checklists and Audits

5S Audit Checklists. Daily or weekly audits to verify Sort, Set in Order, Shine, Standardize, Sustain practices.

Cleaning Schedules. Posted rotation schedules for cleaning tasks, with ownership by area and responsible person.

Physical Cleaning and Organization Tools

Industrial Cleaning Equipment. Floor scrubbers, sweepers, and vacuums appropriate to the factory environment.

Shadow Labels and Foam Inserts. For toolboxes and cabinets to maintain organization and reduce search time.

Pegboards and Modular Racking Systems. For flexible and efficient storage.

Training and Engagement Tools

5S Training Programs. Quick courses or toolbox talks to teach and refresh 5S concepts with your teams.

Kaizen Events Focused on 5S. Engage cross-functional teams to reorganize areas collaboratively.

Before and After Photo Boards. Motivation and recognition to showcase improvements and maintain standards.

Sustainment Tools

Daily Management Boards. Visual boards tracking housekeeping KPIs (audit scores, number of abnormalities corrected, team ownership).

Recognition Programs. Reward teams or individuals for maintaining exemplary housekeeping standards.

Suggestion Systems. Encourage operators to propose organizational improvements.

Just like in life, the way we keep our surroundings reflects how we approach everything else. Discipline in small things builds trust in big things.

No matter how tough the process may seem, never accept a dirty, disorganized workplace. If you want excellence, create the conditions for it. First impressions start with us

Reader Reflection

Housekeeping isn't about cleanliness — it's about pride. People will remember how your workplace looked and felt long after they've forgotten the numbers you achieved.

Ask yourself:

Does my team see housekeeping as everyone's responsibility, including mine?

Do I take action when I see something out of place, or do I walk past it?

What message does our work environment send to visitors, new employees, or customers?

Challenge:

In the next week, find one area in your workplace that's been overlooked — organize, clean, or improve it. Then recognize and thank the people who help keep your workplace safe, organized, and professional. Show that good housekeeping is a reflection of who you are, not just what you do.

Chapter 5. Thinking Outside the Box

"Innovation begins the moment you stop accepting 'that's how we've always done it.'"

There's a saying that goes, "Doing the same thing over and over and expecting a different result is madness." I've seen the truth of that quote many times in my career.

Yes, we value standardization. Yes, reducing variation is critical to quality. But continuous improvement demands something more: the courage to question the status quo and the creativity to imagine something better.

The most transformative changes in the world—across industries, nations, and even personal lives—often begin with a simple question: Is there a better way? Whether it's about speed, quality, efficiency, or innovation, progress depends on our willingness to step outside the familiar and take a different path.

I've found that one of the best ways to broaden our thinking is to expose ourselves to different ideas, different cultures, and different environments. When you immerse yourself in other ways of living, learning, and communicating, you begin to understand that there isn't just one way to solve a problem or reach a goal.

In one company I joined, they had been using the same tools, processes, and routines for years. It had worked well enough to keep the business going, but it was becoming clear that their methods weren't built to compete in a globalized market. Costs were rising, innovation had stalled, and the team lacked fresh perspective.

I introduced concepts like Gemba walks, kaizen events, and standard work systems—well-known in the automotive industry but largely unknown or underutilized in this environment. Initially, some team members dismissed these as "automotive trends," not relevant to their industry. But everything changed when we visited global competitors—plants in Mexico, India, and China.

Many of us had assumed that their low costs were due to lower wages. What we saw instead shocked us: highly automated, efficient, and disciplined operations that went far beyond labor cost savings. The exposure shifted our entire mindset. We began to understand that cost leadership wasn't just about labor—it was about systems, innovation, and bold thinking.

That experience reinforced something I deeply believe: if you don't explore what's out there, your thinking becomes trapped in what you already know.

As a leader, one of my key responsibilities is to challenge the team to think differently—whether drawing from past experience or offering completely radical new ideas. Everything starts by asking:
- Why do we do it this way?
- What if we tried something else?
- What tools, strategies, or models could help us evolve?

Fear of stepping outside the comfort zone is natural. But if we, as leaders, don't challenge ourselves and our teams to explore the "why nots," then we become gatekeepers of stagnation instead of champions of progress.

At the end of the day, we can either follow the path others have laid… Or we can carve out our own.

Which one will help you lead your own revolution?

Practical Ways to Think Outside the Box

Thinking differently is not just a mindset—it's also a discipline. Here are some practical ways I've used or seen successfully applied to help teams think outside the box:

1. Reverse Thinking – Ask the opposite of what you're trying to solve. For example, instead of asking "How can we improve efficiency?", ask "How could we make this process less efficient?" The absurdity of the answers often reveals hidden truths.

2. 'What If' Scenarios – Challenge the team with bold hypothetical questions: "What if we had to deliver the same results with half the resources?" or "What if our main supplier disappeared tomorrow?" These constraints trigger unconventional thinking.

3. Cross-Industry Learning – Look at how other sectors solve similar problems. The medical field, the airline industry, and fast food each have something to teach about systems, safety, speed, or quality.

4. Gemba Walks in Unfamiliar Places – Visit plants, vendors, or even competitors in other regions or countries. Exposure to different workflows, technologies, and cultural mindsets opens new possibilities.

5. No-Limit Brainstorming – Create sessions where budget, roles, and constraints are temporarily removed. Let the team explore wild ideas first, then sort through what's realistic later.

6. Invite Outsiders In – Someone unfamiliar with your process often asks questions that seem simple—but those naive questions often reveal core issues or missed opportunities.

7. First Principles Thinking – Break down problems to their most basic elements. Instead of tweaking a flawed process, ask "What are we really trying to achieve?" and build upward from the goal.

8. 'Kill Your Darlings' Exercise – Ask your team to list what they're most proud of in their current process—and then imagine a world where they can't use those elements. It forces adaptation and reinvention.

9. Role Reversal Exercises – Encourage people to evaluate systems outside of their usual domain. Maintenance critiques training programs. Operators review scheduling systems. Cross-functional insight often leads to innovation.

Each of these methods has helped me or my teams challenge assumptions and spark improvement. Thinking outside the box isn't just about being creative, it's about being brave enough to question what you think you know.

Reader Reflection

Innovation doesn't always start with a big idea — it often begins with a small question: *Why not?*
We all get comfortable doing things the way we've always done them. Familiarity feels safe. But growth lives beyond that comfort zone. The moment we stop questioning "why," we start limiting "what could be."

Ask yourself:

- When was the last time I challenged a long-standing process or tradition at work?
- Do I encourage others to share unconventional ideas, even if they seem risky or unrealistic at first?
- How do I respond when someone challenges *my* way of doing things?

Challenge

In the next week, identify one process, habit, or routine in your team that hasn't changed in years.
Ask your team: *"If we had to start from scratch today, would we still do it this way?"*
Then, listen—really listen—to their ideas. You might not change everything overnight, but you'll have taken the first step toward building a culture that questions, adapts, and grows.

Chapter 6. Teamwork easier said than done.

"Teamwork fails when people protect their territory instead of the mission."

The reality is that we don't apply for jobs to make friends. Our first reason for applying is to fulfill our basic needs - earning a salary to pay for food, housing, transportation, and other essentials. Secondly, we work to achieve our personal and professional goals: becoming a supervisor, manager, director, COO, or even CEO - as far as our skills, hard work, and, why not, a little bit of good luck can take us. I see good luck as an opportunity that presents itself when you're prepared and brave enough to go for it. You can create some of these opportunities, but it's always a challenge to attain them.

While you hold these desires in your heart, you're placed in an environment with many people working towards their own goals. Even though we may be aligned to help the company meet its objectives, those do not replace our personal ones.

Internal competition is human nature. In several companies, I've seen how people chasing their own goals can sometimes hurt the entire department or organization.

I remember one time when a supervisor decided to leave for another company. I've always believed in promoting from within if there are people who meet the required skills and attitude. We decided to promote one of the operators to supervisor, putting him in charge of his former coworkers.

At first, everyone was happy, thinking he would continue to be "one of them." But as responsibilities shifted, it didn't take long for differences to grow, and it became a big issue.

I held a meeting with the new supervisor and the operators. I asked them why they were giving him such a hard time. They said, "Because he's not like he used to be. Now he's asking us to meet goals that are unrealistic."

I reminded them, "The goals haven't changed. They're the same as before. If another supervisor were in charge, expectations would still be the same. So why not support your coworker?" They responded, "We'd rather have someone else."

So, I shared with them a story I heard long ago:

There was a fisherman with two cans of crabs. One can was covered, and the other was left uncovered. The uncovered can contained crabs that knew each other - same background, same community. The covered can had crabs from different parts of the world who didn't know each other.

Another fisherman asked, "Why is one can covered and the other not?"

He replied, "The crabs that know each other always compete between themselves. When one tries to climb out, the others pull him back down, so I don't need to cover them - they'll never get out. But the other can is different. Those crabs don't know each other, they are not competing between themselves, so they come together with a common goal, to leave the can, so they help one another. One crab climb on top of the other, and as soon as one reaches the edge, it pulls the rest up. That's why I keep them covered - otherwise, they'll all be gone before I know it."

I told them, "Sometimes what we envy is what we see every day. We'd rather accept someone from the outside than support the person who worked alongside us for years because deep down, we wonder why they got the recognition instead of us."

This is one of the greatest challenges for a good worker promoted to lead their team. Some succeed in the transition. Some step down to avoid losing friends. And some never even try.

Teamwork should always be encouraged because it strengthens the entire organization. But we must remain aware of how personal goals can sometimes undermine it - not because people don't want to work together, but because each of us has dreams we want to achieve.

Tips for Encouraging Teamwork in a Multicultural Environment

1. Promote Cultural Awareness and Respect: Host cultural learning sessions or informal "culture days." Encourage an environment where differences are viewed as strengths.
2. Establish Clear Communication Norms: Use simple, direct language. Avoid idioms and confirm understanding in a respectful way.
3. Create Inclusive Team Norms: Rotate leadership roles. Make room for different communication and work styles.
4. Set Shared Goals and Values: Build a team identity around purpose and outcomes. Co-create a team charter.
5. Build Psychological Safety: Encourage speaking without fear. Leaders should model humility and invite all opinions.
6. Celebrate Small Wins Together: Acknowledge achievements and allow diverse team members to influence how success is celebrated.
7. Offer Language and Feedback Training: Provide support for intercultural communication and constructive feedback.
8. Lead with Empathy and Curiosity: Ask questions like, "How is this done where you're from?" and encourage personal storytelling.

Rebuilding a Broken Team

Sometimes you walk into a team that's already broken. There's infighting, people throwing each other under the bus, and trust is nowhere to be found. I've seen it more than once, and I can tell you—rebuilding a team like that takes intention, patience, and courage.

The first thing I do is listen. I talk to everyone one-on-one and ask what they think is going on. Most of the time, the issue isn't what people are arguing about, it's something deeper. Hurt pride. A past betrayal. A lack of clarity. You can't fix what you don't understand.

Then, I bring the team together and put the truth on the table. I tell them, 'This is not a functional team. We're fighting more than we're working. That has to change.' It's important to be honest—but also hopeful. Let them know things can get better if they choose to change together.

Next, we reset. We set ground rules. We talk about how we disagree, how we hold each other accountable, and what respect looks like. We shift the focus from 'me vs. you' to 'us vs. the problem.' And we agree that blame games stop today.

Sometimes I'll give people a second chance. But if someone keeps poisoning the team, I deal with it. One person can't be allowed to destroy the culture—even if they're skilled. Respect must come first.

Then we start rebuilding trust through actions, not words. Small wins. Honest conversations. Celebrating when people help each other. Over time, those moments stack up. The team becomes stronger not just because they've succeeded—but because they've survived something difficult together.

If you ever find yourself leading a broken team, don't panic. Lead with courage, consistency, and care. Set the tone. Define the culture. And never forget that even a broken team can become a great one—with the right kind of leadership.

At the end of the day, even the best team can't succeed if the machines they rely on are constantly breaking down. Leadership is about people—but in our world, it's also about systems, reliability, and making sure things don't fall apart when no one's watching. That's where maintenance comes in—not just as a department, but as a mindset.

Reader Reflection

Teamwork doesn't happen by chance — it happens by choice. As leaders, our role is to create an environment where people trust each other enough to share ideas, admit mistakes, and work toward a common goal. Real teamwork begins the moment individuals stop asking, *"Who gets the credit?"* and start asking, *"How can we succeed together?"*

Ask yourself:

- Do I reward collaboration as much as I reward individual achievement?
- How do I respond when team members disagree — do I mediate, take sides, or encourage open dialogue?
- Have I made it clear that success is shared, and that no one wins unless the team wins?

Challenge:

In the next week, look for one opportunity to strengthen collaboration within your team.
It could be by recognizing a group achievement, encouraging cross-department teamwork, or inviting quieter voices into the conversation. Make it clear that in your organization, teamwork isn't just expected — it's valued and celebrated.

What's one action you can take this week to strengthen your team's trust?

Behind every successful team is another team that keeps everything running — maintenance

Chapter 7. Maintenance: From Superheroes to Ghosts

"When maintenance is only noticed during failure, you don't have a maintenance problem—you have a leadership problem."

When we think about maintenance personnel, we picture people who thrive on challenges, those who see something broken and feel compelled to fix it. These are individuals with a diverse set of skills: mechanical, pneumatic, hydraulic, and electrical. They willingly take risks, often working in harsh conditions, and when something breaks down, they become the heroes everyone looks up to for getting it back up and running.

The best of them often carry a hint of cockiness—and that's perfectly fine. When the moment comes, they always deliver.

But as a company, is that what we really need? The answer is yes—but only partly. We absolutely need their skills, their courage, and their determination. But what we truly need is for them to help us prevent and predict failures before they happen.

We need maintenance teams to be so effective that they become almost invisible to the organization—not because they aren't appreciated, but because everything runs smoothly, like a fine Swiss watch. When systems are reliable, heroics aren't required every day.

As a Maintenance Director, this should be your primary goal. However, you must never lose sight of the personalities that make up your team. You need to balance their need for challenges with the company's need for stability. Ideally, 80% of their time should be spent on preventive and predictive tasks, ensuring nothing breaks. The remaining 20% should be dedicated to innovation—working alongside engineering to become heroes of progress, not just daily operations.

Building the Foundation of Reliable Maintenance

In several companies I've worked for, the mentality was to run equipment until it broke down—and of course, it always broke down at the worst possible time. Maintenance would come in to save the day, and everyone would celebrate their heroics. But I started shifting the focus toward preventive and predictive work. Over time, breakdowns became rare.

My gauge of success was when Finance would come to me and ask, "Why do we have so many maintenance people? Nothing ever breaks."

I would smile and tell them, "That's because they're doing exactly what they're supposed to do—working behind the curtain. You may not see them, but trust me, the work is being done."

Then I would share our preventive program with them: specific tasks completed daily, weekly, monthly, semi-annually, and annually.

Achieving this level of reliability requires more than just good intentions. A maintenance manager has many tools at their disposal to ensure reliability and performance:

- **Computerized Maintenance Management System (CMMS):** Tracks maintenance tasks, preventive schedules, spare parts, and historical data.
- **Predictive Maintenance Tools:** Technologies like vibration analysis, infrared thermography, ultrasonic monitoring, and oil analysis detect early-stage issues.
- **Preventive Maintenance Programs:** Checklists and inspections that extend equipment life and reduce breakdowns.
- **Key Performance Indicators (KPIs):** MTBF (Mean Time Between Failures), MTTR (Mean Time To Repair), and OEE (Overall Equipment Effectiveness) provide measurable insights for improvement.
- **Root Cause Analysis (RCA):** Techniques such as 5 Whys, Fishbone, and FMEA address underlying causes of failures.

- **Standard Operating Procedures (SOPs):** Ensure consistency and safety across teams.
- **Condition-Based Monitoring (CBM):** Sensors and IoT (Internet of Things) track equipment health in real time.
- **Cross-Functional Collaboration:** Links maintenance, production, and quality in shared accountability.
- **Spare Parts Management:** Prevents costly downtime without overspending on inventory.
- **Continuous Training:** Keeps technicians current with evolving technology.
- **Compliance Standards:** OSHA and NFPA guide safety and reliability discipline.
- **Visual Management Boards:** Keep communication clear and progress visible.

"If you're just starting, don't let this list overwhelm you. Begin with a CMMS and Root Cause Analysis. When those become habits, the rest will follow."

These are the essential building blocks of maintenance excellence, but remember, tools are only as effective as the people using them. A CMMS that isn't updated daily is just a database. A KPI not discussed with purpose is just a number. What turns systems into results is the discipline, teamwork, and consistency behind them.

If you're starting from scratch, begin with CMMS and Root Cause Analysis. Master those two, and you'll lay the foundation for a proactive culture of reliability.

The Future of Maintenance: From Reactive to Intelligent

In recent years, new technologies have taken maintenance far beyond wrenches and grease guns.
One major leap is the integration of **Supervisory Control and Data**

Acquisition (SCADA) systems with **Artificial Intelligence (AI)**. SCADA collects thousands of data points from machines in real time. AI interprets those data points instantly, identifying subtle anomalies humans might miss.

With this capability, we shift from **scheduled maintenance**—performed on a calendar—to **condition-based maintenance**—performed only when needed. That means fewer unnecessary interventions, reduced costs, and far fewer surprises.

Imagine getting an alert when a hydraulic pump starts vibrating just slightly above normal. You can intervene *before* it fails. That's the power of predictive analytic data and human expertise working hand in hand.

Technology is also transforming how we share expertise. Through **augmented reality (AR)** and remote support tools, an expert halfway across the world can now "look through" a technician's smart glasses, guiding repairs step by step. This reduces response time, builds confidence, and captures tribal knowledge that used to vanish when veterans retired.

The future of maintenance is proactive, intelligent, and collaborative. But technology alone won't fix a broken culture. The foundation remains leadership—leaders who plan, teach, and trust their teams to own reliability.

When Finance and senior leadership see maintenance not as a cost center but as a **strategic advantage**, the conversation changes. Suddenly, maintenance isn't just about fixing machines, it's about sustaining the heartbeat of the company.

Reader Reflection

The best maintenance team is one no one notices—because everything works as it should.

Ask yourself:

- Is your team spending more time reacting or preventing?
- Do you reward firefighting or quiet consistency?
- Does your leadership recognize the unseen work that keeps production running smoothly?

Challenge:

Walk your facility this week. Find one recurring maintenance issue, and instead of patching it again, ask *why* it keeps happening. Solve it permanently. That's how you turn heroes into architects of reliability.

Chapter 8. The Hardest and Easiest Thing to Do—Discipline
"Discipline isn't harsh—it's honest."

One of the biggest challenges as a leader is cultivating discipline throughout an organization—from operators on the floor all the way up to directors. In many North American workplaces, discipline isn't woven into everyday culture. People are often encouraged to be unique, to make their own rules. That mindset can create friction when you're trying to standardize processes, establish procedures, or even maintain something as simple as housekeeping.

I've always believed that the ***minimum expectation is the maximum you will get.*** If you tell people they can arrive five minutes late, most will not come in earlier than that, and some will push the limit further. That's why expectations must be clear and unambiguous: the expectation is to clock in on time. The same principle applies to meetings, and anything else governed by a schedule. Everyone's time is valuable, and respect for that time means being disciplined about schedules and commitments.

Discipline is about standards, but it's also about consistency. I've encountered leaders who effectively say, "Do what I say, not what I do," because they feel exempt from the rules they created. That's a fatal mistake. A leader must lead by example. I would never expect someone to work more than eight hours a day if I weren't willing to do the same; I make a point of working as hard or harder than anyone else, so I'm not seen as a hypocrite. When you live up to the standards you set, no one can legitimately say, ***"You're asking a lot from me, but you don't follow your own rules."***

Consistency also means holding everyone accountable. You can't treat someone differently because of a personal relationship. Once, while interviewing a promising candidate for a supervisor position, I asked him a difficult question. If he got the job, his father would report to him. "If your father makes a mistake serious enough to warrant firing, what would you do?" I asked. He considered the question carefully. "We would investigate whether it was intentional and whether he had the proper training. If the investigation shows negligence, I will treat him like anyone else," he replied. That was the answer I needed. He was promoted, and I moved his father to another department to avoid the situation, but it was a valuable exercise in gauging character and leadership.

Another situation involved team members who wanted to recommend friends for open positions. I always tell them: "If you recommend someone who turns out not to be a good fit, you may lose a coworker and a friend. If you doubt, they will meet expectations, please don't bring them in." This forces them to think twice. Many decide not to recommend anyone; others do, and I like when that happens because they already understand my expectations and what I'll ask of the new hire. So far, those recommendations have turned out well. Asking the question up front seems to secure commitment from both the recommender and the applicant to work hard and succeed.

I don't ask others to do what I'm unwilling to do myself. Early in my career, I had an opportunity for a drafting engineer position. My brother, Alex, was highly skilled in AutoCAD and drafting, so I recommended him. Before doing so, I sat down with him. "I've worked very hard to go from cost engineer to Industrial Engineering Manager," I told him. "You have the skills for this job. You need not just to do a good job but an excellent job, so others don't see you as someone who got a position because of his brother. They will think that at first, no matter what. But then, through hard work, you'll show you earned the role." The Engineering Director told me, "If your brother is half as good as you, I'll hire him." Alex was hired, excelled in his role, and eventually moved on to other opportunities. He succeeded because he understood the expectations and was committed to exceeding them.

These experiences taught me that discipline is not about punishing people; it's about setting clear expectations, leading by example and helping people succeed. Over time, I also learned that leaders can strengthen discipline by following some proven practices. HR research underscores that discipline works best when it "sets and maintains clear expectations for behavior and performance". Most organizations use progressive discipline—starting with a conversation, then a written warning, followed by a final warning or suspension, and only then termination—because addressing minor issues quickly prevents them from becoming major problems. Leaders who visibly follow the rules send a clear message that "no one is above the disciplinary system". A "Just Culture" approach reminds us to investigate the causes of mistakes and ensure similar violations have similar consequences. Effective discipline also requires communication, empathy and support, regular training, timely feedback and thorough documentation.

To summarize, here are the key lessons I've learned about discipline:

Set and communicate clear expectations. Put your standards in writing and review them with everyone so there is no ambiguity about what is acceptable.

Use a progressive approach. Start with a conversation, then a written warning, then a final warning or suspension, and only as a last resort move to termination.

Lead by example. Hold yourself to the same standards as everyone else. When leaders follow the rules, it reinforces the importance of those rules.

Be fair and investigate before acting. Understand the causes of errors and ensure similar violations receive similar consequences.

Communicate and listen. Discuss expectations and consequences openly and work with employees to correct problems rather than surprising them later.

Train and support. Make sure managers know how to apply the policies consistently and give employees the coaching and resources they need to succeed.

Address issues promptly and document everything. Provide feedback immediately after incidents and keep records of conversations and actions.

Discipline, then, is both the hardest and the easiest thing to do. It is hard because it requires self-discipline, consistency and courage. It becomes easy when everyone understands the expectations, sees them modeled at the top, and trusts that the rules apply to everyone the same way. When discipline is handled thoughtfully—through clear communication, fairness, support and consistent action, it fosters a culture where people can thrive.

Reader Reflection

Discipline isn't about control — it's about consistency. It's the quiet force that keeps teams aligned, expectations clear, and standards high even when no one is watching. True discipline starts with self-discipline; you can't demand from others what you don't practice yourself.

Ask yourself:

- Do I model the level of discipline I expect from my team?
- Are my standards clear, consistent, and applied equally to everyone — including myself?
- When someone fails to meet expectations, do I address it promptly and fairly, or do I avoid confrontation?

Challenge:

In the next week, identify one area where discipline has weakened — maybe attendance, deadlines, communication, or follow-up. Reaffirm the standard, communicate it clearly, and hold yourself and others accountable to it. Let your actions remind the team that discipline isn't punishment — it's a shared commitment to excellence.

Chapter 9. Respect at All Levels

"Respect is proven in the small moments, not the speeches."

There's a simple truth I've learned over and over again: how you treat people—all people—says more about your leadership than any title, certification, or post on LinkedIn ever will.

By now, this idea should be so embedded in our professional and personal lives that it no longer needs to be said. And yet, time after time, I've seen leaders at all levels forget it. I've seen organizations proudly display core values on their walls—phrases like "People First" or "Everyone Matters"—only to watch those very same leaders ignore the contributions of janitorial staff, dismiss the voices of frontline workers, or interrupt someone mid-sentence simply because they felt entitled to do so.

Respect is not just a corporate slogan. It is a daily action. It's in the way we listen, acknowledge, include, and value others, especially those who may not have the loudest voices in the room or the fanciest job titles.

What I've Witnessed

In my career, I've walked factory floors where the CEO knew the names of machine operators and said hello to the cleaning crew. I've also been in places where leadership never left their glass offices, too busy with charts and meetings to acknowledge the people making their products or keeping the lights on.

One of the most disappointing things I've seen is when leaders talk a good game in public, especially on social media—promoting inclusion, humility, and cultural values, but act entirely different behind closed doors. It's easy to click "share" on a feel-good quote. It's harder to look someone in the eye, truly listen, and make them feel seen.

Let me be clear: respect isn't about agreeing with everyone or pretending everyone performs equally. It's about recognizing every individual's humanity and dignity, regardless of their job, background, or opinion.

Culture and Respect

Yes, cultures differ. I've worked in the U.S., Mexico, and across multiple international settings, and each place has its own unique norms when it comes to authority, hierarchy, and communication. But no matter where I've gone, the common denominator of effective leadership has always been respect.

Even in places where formality is expected, or where authority is traditionally concentrated at the top, leaders who show genuine regard for their teams consistently inspire better performance, trust, and loyalty.

Why Respect Makes You Stand Out

You don't have to shout to be heard. Sometimes the quietest gesture—thanking someone for their work, asking for input, defending a team member in a difficult meeting—can make the loudest impact.

And here's the truth: when you lead with respect, people remember you. Not just for being effective, but for being worth following. Titles may open doors, but respect builds bridges.

A Personal Story: The Orange and the Opportunity

I remember a moment that deeply impacted me—and it happened early in one of my temporary assignments, when I was asked to oversee operations at a plant in Mexico. The previous boss had left unexpectedly, and I was sent in to stabilize and support the team.

One day, a young HR assistant—bright, well-spoken, and just beginning her professional journey—came to my office and asked me a question that caught me completely off guard:

"Do you want me to do the same thing I did for the previous Plant Manager?"

I paused. My instincts told me something about this question wasn't right, but I needed to understand the environment I had just walked into. So, I asked gently, "What were you doing for him?"

She replied, very matter-of-factly, "He wanted me to peel oranges for him and bring them to his office every day at noon."

I was appalled.

I took a moment to refocus the conversation, and instead of scolding the situation, I turned the attention to her. I asked her about her background, if she had finished her studies. She told me she had recently graduated with a bachelor's degree in human resources. I asked if it had been difficult, and she admitted that while some classes were challenging, she had loved others—and above all, she was proud of having earned her degree.

I smiled and said, "I'm sure your parents are proud too."

Then I answered her question directly:
"No, you don't have to peel oranges for me. You don't even need to do my expense reports—I can do those myself. What I do want is to put your education and potential to good use."

I assured her I would work with the HR Manager to ensure she was given real assignments—tasks that challenged her and helped her grow. I didn't want her to spend her early career doing favors that had nothing to do with the profession she studied so hard for. Instead, I wanted her to be part of improving the company by using the skills she had developed.

Her face lit up.

Before she left my office, I offered one more piece of advice: "In the future, don't let people take advantage of your willingness to help by assigning you tasks that are far below your capability. Your education cost you—and your family—a lot of effort, time, and money. Doing things unrelated to your growth won't serve your long-term career. Know your value. Ask yourself, is this really what I studied for? If the answer is no, speak up. Suggest how you can contribute in ways that match your potential."

Now, was she at fault? Absolutely not. She was doing what she had been told. The fault lies with the leader who asked her to do it.

So, my message is for every manager, supervisor, and director out there: Treat everyone with respect. Even if you started out fetching coffee or doing menial tasks for your boss, ask yourself, did that make you better? Did it help you grow your skills, or would it have been more meaningful to be given real responsibility?

Respect is about recognizing someone's value and making sure your actions match your words. As leaders, we have the power to open doors—or to keep people stuck in the hallway. Choose to open the door.

Another Moment of Respect: The Owner and the Safety Shoes

On another occasion, we had a leadership visit to the production floor, someone entered without the proper safety equipment. He wanted to walk the production floor and meet the teams firsthand.

As he entered one of the areas where safety shoes were required due to the presence of molten metal, an operator quietly approached me with concern.

"He's not wearing safety shoes," the operator said, referring to the upper management visitor.

I turned to him and asked, "Do you believe we all care about safety here?"

"Yes, I do," he responded.

"Then why don't you approach the visitor and tell him? Let him know that here, we all wear safety shoes—not because of the rules alone, but because we care about each other's well-being."

He looked shocked. "No way. He's from Corporate. What if he gets mad or fires me? He can do whatever he wants."

I reassured him, "I think you'll be surprised by his response. Trust me, go talk to him. And if it goes badly, you can say I asked you to do it. I've got your back."

So, with a bit of hesitation, the operator approached the visitor. To his amazement, the Corporate Leader thanked him. He acknowledged the reminder, explained that in his rush to meet the team, he had completely forgotten his safety shoes. He excused himself, returned to change, and came back fully compliant.

Later, in a meeting, the visitor expressed pride in the safety culture of our facility. However, he also admitted disappointment that none of the managers walking with him had spoken up. It was a moment of humility and self-reflection. He accepted responsibility and committed to being more mindful moving forward.

As a token of gratitude, he gave the operator a thank-you card and a small gift. The message was clear: true leadership is being open to feedback and grateful for the people who protect the integrity of your culture—regardless of their title.

Key Takeaways

Respect is an action, not a slogan. It must be practiced daily—not just written in company values or social media posts.

Titles don't define people—character does. Treat everyone, from the owner to the janitor, with the same dignity.
Authenticity matters. Don't be one person in public and another behind closed doors. People notice.
Respect transcends culture. While customs may differ, kindness, listening, and acknowledgment are universal.
Leadership rooted in respect is unforgettable. People may forget what you said, but they will always remember how you made them feel.

One of the greatest compliments a leader can receive is: "He treated everyone with respect." That's the kind of legacy worth leaving.

Reader Reflection

Respect is one of the simplest values to understand—and one of the hardest to live by. It's easy to say "people matter"; it's harder to prove it every day through listening, humility, and fairness. True respect means valuing others not for what they can do for you, but for who they are.

Ask yourself:

- Do I treat everyone—regardless of role, background, or opinion—with the same level of respect?
- When was the last time I genuinely thanked or acknowledged someone whose work often goes unnoticed?
- Do my words about respect match my daily actions, especially when no one is watching?

Challenge:

In the next week, take a moment to recognize someone whose contributions are often overlooked—a janitor, a machine operator, an assistant, or a maintenance technician. Thank them personally and publicly. Let your team see that respect isn't reserved for titles—it's the foundation of your leadership.

Chapter 10. We Always Punish the Best Employees: How to Protect and Empower Top Talent

"If your best people are drowning, it's not dedication—it's mismanagement."

It sounds counterintuitive, almost cruel. But it happens more often than we care to admit we punish our best employees—not intentionally, but systematically. And as leaders, we need to recognize it, stop it, and reverse it.

I once had a technician named Carlos. He was sharp, dedicated, and self-motivated. He never missed a day of work, fixed machines faster than anyone else, and trained new hires without being asked. Naturally, any time something went wrong on a shift, the first reaction was: "Call Carlos." Need someone to stay late? "Carlos can handle it." Equipment failure? "Carlos will figure it out."

What started as recognition of his competence quickly turned into overreliance. Before long, Carlos was burned out and bitter. He confided in me one day:
"I feel like I'm being punished for being good at my job."
That stuck with me.

The Responsibility Gap

As leaders, we must ensure that work is distributed evenly and fairly across the team. Yes, people have different skills and aptitudes—but fairness doesn't mean giving all the tough work to those who can handle it. Too often, the default is to lean on the same person or small group of high performers, especially in times of crisis.

Many times, these individuals:

Have the same job title and same pay as their peers
But they carry much more weight on their shoulders
Take on extra responsibilities without proportional recognition or reward

And while they might receive good performance reviews, compensation often doesn't reflect the added value they bring, especially when companies operate within preset salary bands and budgets. Once someone hits the ceiling, even outstanding performance may not be rewarded fairly.

Meanwhile, employees who avoid challenges or lack initiative might receive support or similar salaries, not because they've earned it, but to keep things "equal" or "stable." This creates frustration, resentment, and disengagement in the very people we depend on most.

Eventually, what we promote—without saying it out loud—is a culture where effort isn't rewarded fairly, and excellence leads to burnout.

The Culture Trap

In many organizations, when someone underperforms, we give them coaching and second chances. But when someone excels, we reward them with... ***more work***. No recognition. No raise. No break. If we're not careful, we start protecting mediocrity while exhausting excellence.

The result?

High performers become disengaged.
Talented people leave.
And those who remain learn to do "just enough."

What Great Leaders Do

We must actively protect and support our best people. Here's how:

Distribute responsibility intentionally – Don't default to the same person for every challenge. Build capability across the team.

Recognize extra effort and skill – Publicly and financially, when possible.

Balance pay with contribution – If two people are paid the same, they should contribute at a similar level—or the system needs reevaluation.

Refuse to enable imbalance – Don't compensate poor performance with support at the expense of your best people.

Create a fair development path – Ensure high performers see opportunities for growth, not just more pressure.

A Lesson in Fairness

One day, I met with a production supervisor who was furious that his best operator wanted a day off during a busy week. "How can he leave when we need him most?" he asked.

I calmly replied, "And when does he get to need us?"

That moment changed his perspective—and mine. Fairness isn't about treating everyone the same. It's about giving each person what they need to thrive.

Closing Reflection

Your best employees are not infinite resources. They are human. They are loyal, committed, and capable—but even they have a breaking point. When we fail to reward their effort and allow imbalance to grow, we push them away.

Leadership isn't just about results. It's about protecting those who deliver them. Don't punish your best elevate them.

Reader Reflection

Great leaders don't just protect their best people from burnout — they build a system where excellence is recognized and rewarded fairly.

Ask yourself:

- Am I unconsciously giving more work to high performers while underperformers get by?
- How often do I recognize or reward extra effort?
- Do my team members believe that excellence leads to opportunity, or to exhaustion?
- Am I creating growth paths for top talent, or just piling on responsibility?

Challenge:

Choose one high performer on your team. Instead of giving them another task, find a way this week to **recognize, support, or develop** them. It could be public praise, a fair raise request, a learning opportunity, or simply respecting their need for balance.

Chapter 11. Not Making a Decision Is Also a Decision

"Delaying a decision is choosing the outcome you least want."

One of the main roles of leadership is to make decisions. Some are relatively simple: Should we work overtime to make up for lost production hours? Others are much harder: Should we lay off personnel due to a lack of sales and no new orders coming in?

Regardless of their size, decisions always carry weight. They impact the company, the people working in it, the customers depending on it, and the suppliers connected to it. Leaders are constantly under pressure to make the "right" decision, and that pressure can cause hesitation. Many stall, waiting for perfect data, complete clarity, or the ideal scenario that never arrives.

The truth is, sometimes there is no time. A decision must be made with incomplete information, and waiting too long can be worse than acting and making a mistake. One choice can preserve the rewards you've worked hard to enjoy — or it can put your own position at risk.

As you climb higher in leadership, your direct interaction with day-to-day tasks decreases, but your responsibility to take decisive action increases. You don't always get the luxury of certainty. That's the price of leadership.

And here's the hard truth: if you don't like the pressure and uncertainty that comes with decision-making, leadership may not be for you. And that is perfectly fine. Some people are happier as followers — doing their jobs well, being told what needs to be done, and focusing on execution rather than direction.

But if you are in a leadership role, indecision is not neutrality. By failing to act, you're allowing circumstances to decide for you — and ***those consequences are still yours to own.***

A Lesson from Experience

Throughout my career, I've noticed how different cultures and individuals react to decision-making. Of course, not everyone is the same, but I've seen environments where leaders struggled to act unless they had 120% certainty that the data was correct. While they kept analyzing and double-checking, nothing was happening — no decision, no movement — and performance began to suffer.

At one company, we faced a sales crisis. The market had shifted, and our pricing was 15–20% higher than competitors. Customers were rejecting our offers. The CFO, however, was firm on one rule: never accept a profit margin below a set number. On paper, that looked disciplined. In reality, it meant no new business was coming in. The high margin work we had wasn't enough to cover our fixed costs like depreciation, and every month the pressure rose.

Finally, I went to him and laid it out plainly:

"Do you want 35% of nothing, or 10% of a million?"

If we continued on the same path, we were going to run ourselves out of business. I argued that we needed to adapt — take some jobs at lower margins, even at breakeven, to keep our costs covered and protect our people. The more sales we brought in, the more we could spread out labor costs. That meant less idle time, fewer people sent home, and lower risk of losing talent. Because once people leave, you're not just replacing them — you're absorbing the cost of training, scrap, and lost efficiency.

In the end, I made the decision to push for lower-margin work. It wasn't the perfect scenario, but it gave us time, kept our workforce stable, and protected the future of the company.

That experience taught me something important: indecision, disguised as waiting for more data, is often more dangerous than making a less-than-perfect decision with the information you already have.

Cultural Tendencies and Gut Feelings

I've also seen that in places like Mexico and the United States; leaders are often more comfortable making decisions with 70–80% of the information. Some call it a "gut feeling," but in reality, it's the confidence to move forward knowing that adjustments can always be made along the way.

A decision is rarely final. Once you act, you can make small tweaks, course-corrections, or refinements to get closer to where you need to be. And if it turns out to be the wrong decision, you learn for the next one.

There's a saying I believe in strongly:

"If you don't make mistakes, it's because you never make decisions."

Leaders must embrace this truth. Perfection isn't the goal — progress is.

Supporting Others to Decide

As a leader, you also don't want every decision to bottleneck on you. If all choices — big or small — wait for your approval, the organization stalls. Leadership is not about being the only decision-maker; it's about creating other leaders.

That means encouraging your team members to make decisions themselves, giving them the confidence that you will support their judgment. When mistakes happen — and they will — don't punish them for trying. Instead, ask them to find the solution to correct the problem.

Leadership Insight: The $1.5 Million Mistake

Earlier in my career, I made a mistake that could have cost the company $1.5 million if it had reached production. Thankfully, I caught it in time and worked quickly to correct the issue before it became a reality.

What mattered most wasn't that the mistake happened — it was how I responded. I didn't walk away, I didn't hide, and I didn't try to shift the blame. I took responsibility, fixed the problem, and learned from it.

That experience shaped how I lead today. Mistakes aren't always fatal to your career — in fact, they can become defining growth moments. As leaders, our role is to help our teams see errors not as failures, but as opportunities to improve. The goal isn't perfection, but resilience: the ability to face challenges, solve problems, and come back stronger.

The Lesson from Pancho Villa

There's an old story in Mexico about leadership that comes from Pancho Villa. At times, his men would capture someone who wasn't part of their group and bring him forward with uncertainty: Was this person a spy? An enemy infiltrator? Or simply an innocent caught in the wrong place?

They would ask Villa, "What should we do with him?" His response was decisive, even brutal:
"If you don't know who he is, just shoot him — then we'll find out."

Extreme as it sounds, his reasoning was clear. If he was wrong, he might have lost one supporter — and he had thousands. But if he was right, he could prevent an infiltrator from sharing plans that might cost him his mission, his army, and his own life.

The story isn't about endorsing violence — it's about illustrating the danger of indecision when lives, missions, or companies are on the line. Villa knew that hesitation could cost far more than the risk of being wrong.

Key Takeaways & Practical Steps

Indecision is still a decision — but usually the worst one. By not acting, you allow circumstances to dictate the outcome.

Act with 70–80% of the information. Waiting for 100% certainty will paralyze progress. Use your best judgment, move forward, and adjust as needed.

Frame the stakes clearly. Like asking, "Do we want 35% of nothing or 10% of a million?" — sometimes simplifying the options makes the right choice obvious.

Balance data and instinct. Data is valuable, but don't underestimate experience, intuition, and context in guiding decisions.

Accept imperfection. A decision can always be corrected, improved, or adapted. Inaction cannot.

Support your team in decision-making. Don't centralize all authority. Empower others, back them up, and help them grow into leaders themselves.

Treat mistakes as tuition. If an error is made, require a corrective solution — don't let people walk away from it. Growth comes from responsibility.

Manage the pressure. Remember that not every decision defines your entire career. Learn from outcomes — good or bad — and use them to grow as a leader.

Courage over certainty. True leadership isn't about knowing everything; it's about having the courage to act when others freeze.

"The only wrong decision is no decision at all. Leadership isn't about knowing everything — it's about having the courage to act."

Reader Reflection

Indecision may feel safe, but it often carries the highest cost. Every time we delay a decision, we also delay progress, solutions, and growth. Great leaders don't wait for perfect conditions—they act with the best information they have and adjust along the way. Courage doesn't mean you're always right; it means you're willing to take responsibility when you're wrong.

Ask yourself:

- Do I hesitate to decide because I fear being wrong, or because I truly need more clarity?
- How often do I let opportunities pass while waiting for perfect data?
- Do I empower my team to make decisions, or do they wait for me because I haven't given them the confidence to act?

Challenge:

In the coming week, identify one important decision you've been postponing—big or small.
Gather the information you already have, trust your experience, and take action. Then, reflect on the outcome. What did you learn about your instincts, your leadership, and your tolerance for risk?

Remember: leadership is not about avoiding mistakes; it's about moving forward despite uncertainty.

Chapter 12. Estimating and Budgeting: The Numbers Behind Leadership Decisions

"Budgets don't lie—leaders just have to be willing to listen."

When people think of leadership, they often picture speeches, vision, or decision-making in boardrooms. But in manufacturing, I learned very early that leadership also lives in the numbers—specifically in how well you can estimate and budget. These are the hidden forces behind strategy, because no matter how bold your vision may be, if the numbers don't work, the idea will never leave the page.

My First Lesson: Becoming a Cost Engineer

As I shared in The Road of a Dreamer, my first role in the manufacturing industry was as a Cost Engineer. Different companies call it by different names, but the task is the same: determine how much a part will cost to produce and propose a pricing structure that not only covers costs but also generates profit.

At the time, I quickly realized this was more than "crunching numbers." It was about understanding every step of the process, every resource required, and every risk that could affect profitability. Here's what I learned went into a strong cost estimate:

- **A complete Bill of Materials (BOM):** This is the foundation. It lists every raw material, every purchased component, and every consumable item needed to produce the part. Without a solid BOM, the estimate collapses.
- **Labor and time studies**: You must calculate how much time and manpower it will take to assemble and process all the components. A missed operation or underestimated cycle time can shift the entire cost model.
- **Scrap and setup allowances:** Processes often generate non-sellable parts—setup pieces required for approval, destructive samples for testing, or rejected scrap. These must be included, or else costs will be understated.
- **Outside services:** Some operations require external suppliers—for heat treating, coating, machining, or specialized test-

ing. These costs include not only the supplier's invoice but also shipping, handling, and any scrap they generate.
- **Variable and fixed costs:** Beyond the tangible items, there are the operational costs—equipment depreciation, maintenance, electricity, gas, and water. These may be calculated by finance, but a good engineer must understand their impact.

Once all of these items are captured, *the sales team usually sets the final selling price*, balancing company profitability with market competitiveness. Sometimes the market dictates the margin available, and the best you can do as an engineer is to ensure that your estimate reflects reality so the business can make informed choices.

The Hidden Risk: One Small Omission

I also learned how dangerous even a small oversight could be. As I later shared in *The Road of a Dreamer*, I once faced with what could have been a **$1.5 million mistake.** A single omission in my estimate, when multiplied by the projected sales volume, could have cost the company dearly. Fortunately, corrective actions prevented the loss, but the experience marked me permanently.

It taught me that attention to detail is not optional, it is survival. In leadership, one miscalculated assumption can ripple through production, pricing, and strategy, multiplying its impact far beyond the original error.

Leadership Beyond the Estimate

As a leader, it is critical to understand not only how to produce but also **how much your manufacturing process truly costs.** You must know the assumptions that were made when a project was first quoted and use them as a baseline for performance. This becomes the minimum expectation—the point of reference to measure if reality aligns with what was promised.

Once the process is stabilized to meet those assumptions, the next step is improvement: How can we perform better than expected? Without this reference point, you are essentially flying blind—lacking a true measure of whether you are meeting, exceeding, or falling short of the financial targets.

This is not only about the standards set by engineering, but about a broader understanding of the entire cost structure tied to a component. Something as "simple" as an increase in transportation costs, for example, can erase expected profits.

That is why leadership must extend beyond the walls of the manufacturing floor. Everything—from labor and scrap to utilities, logistics, and market fluctuations—affects the bottom line of the organization. Your role as a leader is to stay aware, connect these dots, and take proactive actions to control costs. And if possible, to improve results beyond the baseline, creating value that strengthens both the operation and the business.

From Estimates to Leadership Scorecards

In my current role, I have taken those early lessons and built them into a **leadership scorecard** a tool that helps me monitor every aspect of the organization. But I have always viewed this scorecard in a **monetary way**. Every number tells a financial story, and every deviation from the quote has consequences for profitability.

For example, I track quality not only by incidents per million but also by **scrap dollars versus sales**, calculating the percentage and validating it against the original cost assumptions. I measure **labor costs** versus quoted, as well as **efficiency and equipment utiliza-**

tion versus quoted. Each of these metrics tells me whether we are inside the range of our original assumptions, outside of it, or trending in a concerning direction.

This clarity allows us to put targeted plans in place. If a cost driver is off track, we focus on correcting it. If an assumption used during quoting turns out to be incorrect, we adjust it for future quotes. And if the impact is significant, the sales team may need to engage with the customer to revise pricing. For instance, tariffs are something that might not have been included in the original quote but can dramatically increase costs on imported materials. In such cases, transparency with the customer becomes critical to maintaining both profitability and trust.

By using a scorecard approach, I can connect the dots between **estimating, budgeting, execution, and leadership**. Numbers are not just abstract values, they are signals that guide decisions, reveal risks, and show opportunities for improvement. More importantly, they ensure that we are never flying blind but always leading with both vision and financial discipline.

Lessons Learned

- **Start with the details.** A strong BOM and process review are the backbone of any estimate.
- **Don't ignore the hidden costs.** Scrap, setups, logistics, and outside services can make or break profitability.
- **Partner with finance and sales.** Cost engineers build the foundation, but sales must balance price with market realities.
- **Attention to detail saves millions.** One small omission can multiply into a massive loss.
- **Budgets are leadership tools.** They don't just track money—they communicate priorities and discipline.

- **Leaders must monitor assumptions.** Performance against the quote is the compass for improvement.
- **Scorecards connect vision to numbers.** They show whether the organization is truly delivering what was promised.

Closing Reflection

Numbers alone do not inspire people. They will never replace vision, passion, or the human side of leadership. But without them, even the boldest dream risks becoming an illusion. Estimating and budgeting give dreams a foundation; they show what it takes to turn an idea into reality.

As leaders, we cannot be afraid of the numbers. We must own them, question them, and use them as a compass. When we understand the costs, the assumptions, and the impact of our decisions, we gain not just control but credibility. And credibility is what transforms a dream into something others are willing to follow.

Because in the end, dreamers who lead are not defined only by their vision, but by their ability to align that vision with discipline, detail, and financial truth. That is how we build organizations that not only dream but endure.

Reader Reflection

Numbers tell a story, but it's up to leaders to interpret it and act.

Ask yourself:

- Do I know the assumptions behind my budgets, or do I just accept the numbers as given?
- Am I tracking not just results, but also the gaps between estimated and actual performance?

- How transparent am I with my team or customers when costs or conditions change?
- Do I use numbers as a tool to inspire confidence, or as a weapon to create fear?

Challenge:

Pick one current project or budget. Compare the original assumptions to actual results so far. Identify at least one place where reality has shifted — and decide what conversation or adjustment needs to happen because of it.

Chapter 13. The Power of Communication and Feedback (as a Growth Tool)

"Most conflicts come from what was assumed, not what was said."

Communication: The Core Skill of Leadership

One of the questions I am often asked by managers is: *What is the most important skill a leader needs to be successful?*
My answer has always been the same: ***communication***.

A leader must be able to convey ideas, goals, and expectations in a way that is not only clear but inspiring. True communication goes beyond knowledge transfer—it sparks belief. When people understand and believe in a goal, they commit to making it happen.

This is why goals must be both **challenging and attainable**. If a goal is too easy, there is no sense of achievement; if it is impossible, the result is frustration and demotivation. A leader's responsibility is to assess what can be accomplished with the tools, processes, and team available, and then set goals that stretch but don't break the team. Every time a team achieves one of these goals, it matures and becomes ready for a bigger challenge.

Shared Ownership of Goals

The way goals are communicated is just as important as the goals themselves. When people are involved in shaping them, their commitment grows. Shared ownership creates energy and accountability. A leader who simply dictates objectives may achieve compliance, but a leader who engages the team in building them earns commitment.

I have seen this play out in powerful ways. At one company, our team achieved the **Supplier Quality Award for seven consecutive years**. That was not luck, it was the result of everyone understanding and committing to quality, supported by the right tools and the right people. At another company, the team went years without a lost-time accident. Why? Because every employee knew they were responsible not only for their own safety but also for their teammates'.

These are not results you can enforce by rules alone. They are the outcomes of cultures built on communication—leaders who believed these results were possible and made their teams believe it too.

Multiplying Leadership Through Communication

To sustain these cultures, communication must happen at every level:

- **As a group**, through monthly or quarterly meetings where progress and priorities are shared.
- **One-on-one**, where leaders work closely with their direct managers to align expectations and motivate them.

This layered communication creates a ripple effect: leaders empowering managers, who in turn empower their teams. One of the biggest mistakes a leader can make is to become the sole source of authority. If everyone believes only *you* are making the decisions, you have failed. But if your team members see their managers as the ones driving results, you have succeeded—not only in achieving goals, but in **creating more leaders.**

Continuous Feedback: The Compass for Growth

Feedback is not a one-time event—it is a continuous compass that keeps individuals and teams aligned. One of the biggest struggles many leaders face is providing honest evaluations to their managers. The easiest path is to say, *"You're exceeding expectations."* Everyone likes to hear that, and it avoids uncomfortable conversations. But this approach is misleading and dangerous.

If someone is only meeting expectations—or worse, not meeting them at all—those conversations need to happen. And they need to happen in a **constructive** way, as often as necessary, until the person clearly understands what is expected. The last thing a leader wants is for a team member to be surprised. Nothing damages trust more than someone believing they were performing well, only to later learn their results were falling short.

Yes, these conversations are not easy but delaying them only compounds the problem. Addressing performance gaps **early and directly** gives people the opportunity to adjust and succeed.

The higher your responsibilities, the more tempting it is to let feedback slip through the cracks. Meetings, travel, and urgent decisions consume time and energy. But a true leader makes time to sit with their team, share how things are going, and align expectations for the week ahead. A five- or ten-minute check-in can make the difference between drifting off course and staying on track.

The same principle applies with direct managers and leaders. Leaders must not only monitor results but also pay attention to signs of stress, burnout, or behavior changes. Sometimes the feedback needed is not about performance numbers but about balance, focus, and resilience. Helping leaders get back on the right trajectory is just as important as correcting technical performance.

Continuous feedback, when done with honesty and empathy, prevents surprises, builds accountability, and keeps both individuals and organizations aligned toward success.

A Lesson from Feedback: Knowing Myself

Throughout my career, I've received several personality assessments, one of the most common being the **DiSC profile**. These tools measure how you think, interact, and respond under pressure. My results have almost always described me as an *implementer*: someone who focuses on a task with laser precision and pushes until the job is done.

That assessment was accurate. I've always been task-driven, but that strength came with blind spots. One evaluation in particular pointed out that I seemed too focused on results and didn't always consider the feelings or struggles of people around me. My conversations were often purely about projects, numbers, and results. To others, I came across as cold, distant, and uninterested in people.

At first, the feedback stung. But it was true—not because I didn't care about people, but because my natural style prioritized results. I realized that while I couldn't change who I was, I could **balance myself by partnering with those who had strengths I lacked**. That's when I began building strong partnerships with human resources managers. I learned to share my plans and approaches with them first, to hear how my message might be received. Their feedback helped me temper my directness, adding empathy without losing focus.

These became some of the most valuable relationships of my career. By listening and applying their feedback, I became not only a more effective leader, but also a more human one. The lesson was clear: **feedback is not just about performance; it's about self-awareness.**

Closing Reflection

Communication and feedback are not just leadership tasks; they are the lifelines of growth. Clear communication creates alignment, shared ownership builds belief, and continuous feedback sustains progress. And when leaders are humble enough to listen—even when the feedback is uncomfortable—they unlock a deeper level of growth in themselves and their teams.

When leaders embrace these tools, they don't just manage results; they **multiply leadership** at every level of the organization. That is how cultures of safety, quality, and performance are built—not through control, but through communication and feedback that inspire people to own the vision and carry it forward.

Reader Reflection

Take a moment to think about the quality of communication within your team.

Do your people clearly understand not only what needs to be done, but *why* it matters?
Are you creating the space for others to speak up, share ideas, and challenge your own assumptions?
Consider the last time you provided feedback—was it balanced, timely, and rooted in helping someone grow, or did it come only after a problem surfaced?

Great communication isn't just about delivering messages; it's about building trust. Feedback isn't criticism, it's a sign that you believe in someone's potential to do better. Reflect on how your words and actions are shaping the level of openness and confidence within your organization.

Challenge for the Reader

In the coming week, choose **two people** on your team or in your professional circle:

- One with whom communication feels effortless.
- One with whom it feels strained or distant.

For each, schedule a short conversation—not to review performance, but to *listen*. Ask what's working, what isn't, and what they need from you as a leader.

Then, commit to these three actions:

1. **Clarify** one key goal or expectation that might not be fully understood.
2. **Offer** one piece of constructive feedback that will help them grow.
3. **Invite** feedback for yourself—ask, "What can I do better to support you?"

Repeat this regularly. As you build this rhythm of two-way communication, you'll find that feedback becomes less of an event and more of a habit, a leadership reflex that fuels trust, performance, and growth.

Chapter 14. Promote Yourself—There's Nothing Wrong With That

"If you don't speak for your work, someone else will speak over it."

Since very early in my life, I learned that it is important what you do—but it is also important that people know you did it. In a way, this book and The Road of a Dreamer are part of that. They are my way of sharing with the world a story that many people would not otherwise know—even people close to me who had no idea how I grew up, the struggles I faced, or how I led at work.

Now, readers of my first book know about both the challenges and the happy moments of my life. And the same principle applies at work: if you don't share your accomplishments, people may never know about them.

Recognition is not just about ego. When someone tells you "Great job," it makes you feel good—but more importantly, it drives you to keep getting better. Small accomplishments matter, and they should be recognized, because they fuel momentum. But here's the truth: everyone is busy, and nobody has time to track every single thing that you or your team are doing. That's why you have to make it a deliberate task—for yourself and for your teams—to let others know what you did and the results you achieved.

Promoting yourself is not arrogance; it's about making sure your contributions are visible, your voice is heard, and your path forward is clear. It's not about inflating your importance—it's about making sure your value is recognized.

I have seen many talented people stay in the shadows because they thought speaking up would be considered bragging. Meanwhile, others, sometimes with less substance, stepped forward, highlighted their work, and received the promotions, the opportunities, and the trust of leadership. In the end, visibility matters as much as capability.

Promoting Yourself the Right Way

Promoting yourself isn't about exaggerating or taking credit for things you didn't do. It's about:

Highlighting Results: Clearly communicating what has been achieved, why it matters, and how it contributes to the larger goals.
Sharing Credit: Elevating your team members when you talk about results—because leadership is never a solo act.
Telling the Story: Framing the work in a way that executives, peers, or even subordinates can understand its importance.
Positioning for Growth: Letting others know where you want to go next so they can see you as a candidate for bigger challenges.

Promoting Others Is Also Your Job

One of the things leaders sometimes forget is that they are responsible for everything that happens in their areas of responsibility. That means it's not only okay but necessary to let people who report to you go and share their ideas. In fact, I would say it's part of your job to encourage it—because they are a reflection of you and your leadership.

Some leaders, out of insecurity, hold back their people. They worry that if someone else shines, it will put their own position in jeopardy. But here's the truth: if your success depends on stopping someone else from growing, then you need to look at yourself and ask how you can continue to grow. ***Leadership is not about limiting others; it's about multiplying leaders.***

One of my greatest satisfactions has been seeing people who once worked for me rise to roles like Director or even President. Yes, they had the skills and the drive—but I know I helped them by not getting in the way, by encouraging them to show their accomplishments directly to management.

A practical way I did this was by asking my team to present their results and improvements during monthly or quarterly plant-wide meetings. These presentations were often attended by executives, sometimes even the owners of the company. The truth is, senior management already knew about the successes or challenges we were facing—I had already communicated those. But these moments were about letting the people doing the work own it, present it, and explain not only the results but also the challenges they had overcome.

This practice gave higher management confidence that the organization wasn't built on one person but on a strong team of individuals working hard to get things done. And for the team members, it was a confidence-building opportunity to grow their own leadership presence.

Sharing Builds Legacy

Sharing your experiences doesn't just help you remember them—it creates a legacy. If even one person learns from something you've lived through, then you've left behind something that will not fade, even after you are gone. The same way I've learned lessons from historical figures—sometimes not remembering exactly who said it or where it was written but remembering the lesson itself—your stories can live on in the actions of others.

During the promotion of The Road of a Dreamer, I sat down with different people who had read the book. One of them, Rafael Sepúlveda, shared a story with me that I had actually forgotten. Years ago, he made a mistake by using the wrong fixture placement during heat treatment, which distorted the parts and caused serious issues. He told me he came to me ready to take full ownership—and even ready to quit.

Instead, I told him, "No—you're not quitting. Now you have to go fix it." And that's what he did. He went to the customer, worked to solve the problem, and made sure it never happened again.

Rafael told me that after reading about my own story—the $1.5 million dollar mistake I almost made—he saw the parallel. He realized that I had faced similar situations, and instead of giving up, I had chosen to fix them. He told me that when I challenged him to take the same approach, it marked him for life. He said, "I will carry this lesson for the rest of my life."

I didn't even remember the story until Rafael brought it up, but it reminded me of something powerful: as leaders, we create patterns. We shape the way others respond to challenges. And when those patterns take root, we're not just solving problems, we're building new leaders who follow the same path.

Key Takeaways

Promoting yourself is not arrogance, it's ownership of your value.
Execution and communication go hand in hand; results without visibility are often invisible.
Leaders must also promote their people, not hold them back.
Insecurity limits growth—true leadership is measured by how many leaders you create.
Use structured opportunities (like plant-wide or quarterly meetings) to let your people present their work and challenges directly to higher management.
Recognition builds confidence, and confidence fuels growth.
Sharing your stories builds legacy—the lessons outlast the storyteller.

That is why I wrote The Road of a Dreamer: because stories matter, and the lessons we share become the seeds of future leaders.

Reader Reflection

Think about the last time you shared your accomplishments—or helped someone else share theirs.

Did you hesitate out of fear of being seen as arrogant? Or did you take pride in your contribution and the growth it represented?

Many talented professionals stay invisible not because they lack results, but because they avoid recognition. True humility is not about silence, it's about honesty. If you and your team are doing meaningful work, letting others know is not self-promotion, it's stewardship. You're showing what's possible when people take ownership and deliver results.

Reflect on how you communicate your value today. Do others understand the impact you and your team are creating? Do you give your people opportunities to shine? Visibility is not vanity—it's the bridge between effort and opportunity.

Challenge for the Reader

In the next 30 days, take deliberate action to **make your work and your team's success visible**:

1. **Document three achievements** from the past quarter—large or small—that made a difference in performance, safety, quality, or culture.
2. **Share these accomplishments** with your leadership team or peers in a professional, factual way. Focus on impact, not ego.

3. **Spotlight someone else's contribution.** Encourage one of your team members to present a result, improvement, or lesson learned in the next meeting.
4. **Start a "Recognition Habit."** End each week by thanking one person who demonstrated leadership, creativity, or resilience.

When you consistently recognize effort, your own and others'—you build confidence, credibility, and momentum. Over time, you'll find that promoting your work isn't about being noticed, it's about **building a legacy that others can see, learn from, and continue.**

Chapter 15. Sales Is Not About Selling — It's About Solving a Problem

"Sales starts when you stop talking and start understanding."

Most people hear the word *sales* and immediately think of pressure, targets, or someone trying to convince them to buy something they don't need.
But the truth is, **sales are not about selling — it's about solving a problem.**

Every good leader, engineer, or operator is in sales, whether they realize it or not. We all sell ideas, solutions, and confidence every day. We sell trust when we ask people to follow us. We sell change when we propose a new process. We sell belief when we promise that things can get better.

Sales, at its core, is not a department, it's a mindset. And for leaders, that mindset makes the difference between being heard and being followed.

Everyone Is in Sales

Early in my career, I thought sales were for people in suits with briefcases — the ones who spent their time visiting customers and talking about prices. I was an engineer; my job was to fix machines, not to sell. But I quickly learned that to make progress, I had to *sell ideas* every single day.

When I wanted to implement a new maintenance system, I had to convince the plant manager that it wasn't just another cost — it was an investment in uptime and safety. When I proposed replacing a press that constantly failed, I wasn't just asking for capital approval; I was selling a solution that would reduce downtime, improve quality, and protect our reputation.

What I learned from those experiences is simple: **leadership and sales share the same foundation — trust and problem-solving.**

When Sales Becomes Responsibility

I have found myself leading sales efforts not because I wanted to, but because I needed to.
There are usually two main reasons this happens.

The first is when I start seeing a trend — low sales coming into the plant due to an economic downturn, the end of a product's life cycle, or inefficiencies that make some customers look elsewhere.
The second is when we have worked hard to improve our processes and efficiency, and suddenly we have **open capacity** that needs to be filled.

Sometimes, the sales team isn't fully in tune with what's happening on the production floor.
But one of my biggest responsibilities as a leader has always been to make sure **we provide steady work for our people**.
When I notice these patterns, I feel a deep sense of urgency to bring in new projects — not to chase numbers, but to protect jobs and preserve the years of investment we've made in training our people.

Layoffs are painful — financially and emotionally. Every time you lose a skilled employee, you don't just lose a worker; you lose knowledge, morale, and part of the company's heart. These ups and downs are costly not only to the company's profits, but to the human motivation of those who keep the plant running. Everyone wants stability — steady work, steady pay, and the pride of knowing their contribution matters.

Unfortunately, sales teams often aren't part of these operational realities. Their urgency is driven by commissions and quarterly targets, while ours is driven by **the immediate impact of empty workstations and worried faces**.

That's why I often get personally involved — to find ways to prevent both a reduction in personnel and a loss in profitability.

When that happens, the first thing I do is reach back to our customers. I check in — not to sell, but to understand. Are their needs being met? Do they have new projects we can help with? Are there services or products we can offer that fit their changing demands? Sometimes, those simple conversations open new doors. A small quote request can turn into a larger collaboration.
We share ideas — *they know their processes, and we know ours.* Together, we look for ways to improve.

On several occasions, these interactions have led to unexpected opportunities — like hosting training sessions for their engineers or supporting them in areas outside our core business. The revenue from those training courses is often minimal, but what matters more is the relationship we build. We become partners, not just suppliers. And that kind of trust often leads to continuous collaboration and long-term growth.

Sometimes Sales Are Built from Helping a Customer

Sometimes sales are born not from a presentation or a quote, but from a moment of genuine help.

I remember one time receiving a call from a maintenance manager who was clearly stressed. His critical piece of equipment had gone down, shutting his entire operation. He reached out to me because he knew we had similar equipment at our plant and might have the spare part he needed. After checking, I confirmed that we did have it — and time was everything.

We quickly made a plan. I searched for flights between our cities and called one of my maintenance technicians to explain the situation: *we have a customer in trouble; they need a part today — would you be willing to fly there and deliver it in person?*

He had never flown before, so it became both an adventure and a mission of service. I booked his round-trip flight, personally drove him to the airport, and handed him the spare part. A few hours later, he landed on the other side of the country, where the maintenance manager met him at the terminal. He handed over the part, and the manager rushed back to install it and restart his facility.

That evening, my technician enjoyed a nice dinner before flying back home the same night — tired but proud.

The next morning, the maintenance manager called to thank me personally. He told me the equipment was back up and running and that our help had prevented a major production loss. He immediately reimbursed the travel costs, paid for the spare part, and even added a bonus for our company as recognition of our service.

That event was never part of our sales plan or business model. But through that simple act of helping, we didn't just sell a part, we solved a problem. And in doing so, **we earned a long-term partner** who knew we would come through whenever they needed us.

Solving the Right Problem

One of the biggest mistakes I've seen companies make is believing they need to sell harder, when in reality they need to **listen better**. Too often, people focus on presenting features, prices, and statistics without ever understanding what the customer — or the team — really needs.

I remember visiting a customer who was frustrated with our delivery times. Everyone assumed the issue was logistics — trucks, routes,

or scheduling. But after listening carefully, we discovered the real issue wasn't late delivery; it was *lack of communication.*
They didn't know when to expect the product, and that uncertainty caused them to plan around us. We solved the problem not with a new process, but with a weekly update system. The result? More trust and more business.

That lesson stayed with me. When you take the time to understand the *real* problem, the sale happens naturally. You're no longer convincing — you're connecting.

The Ethics of Sales in Leadership

Selling is easy when you don't care about consequences. But **real sales, the kind built on integrity, takes courage.**

There have been moments in my career when walking away from a deal felt like a loss — but it was the right thing to do. I've learned that you don't win by closing every opportunity; you win by keeping your word.

I once had a customer who wanted a price, we simply couldn't deliver without cutting corners. Instead of forcing it, I told them honestly, *"I'd rather lose your order than lose your trust."*
Months later, that same customer called back — not because of price, but because they knew we stood for something.

When you lead with ethics, people remember you long after the contract expires.

Building Trust Before Selling Anything

The best salespeople — and the best leaders — don't start by talking. They start by listening. They don't rush to prove a point; they earn the right to be heard.

When I led teams through change, I didn't sell them the idea of change with words — I showed them results.
Once, when implementing a predictive maintenance program, there was skepticism everywhere. People thought it was "just another initiative." But after a few months, when they saw fewer breakdowns, fewer call-ins, and smoother operations, I didn't have to convince anyone anymore. They became the advocates themselves.

That experience taught me something I'll never forget **when trust is built, you don't have to sell — people buy into you.**

The Leader as a Problem Solver

Leadership, in its purest form, is about solving problems.
The same is true for sales.

When you align the two, you stop chasing approval and start creating value.
In manufacturing, we often look at numbers — efficiency, cost, scrap, and delivery. But behind every metric is a problem waiting to be solved. The leader who learns to "sell" their solution in a way others can believe in is the one who moves organizations forward.

I've seen leaders push ideas that looked great on paper but failed because they didn't connect with the real issue. I've also seen small ideas succeed because they were framed around a genuine need. The difference wasn't strategy — it was empathy and communication.

The Human Connection

At the end of the day, selling is not about persuasion — it's about people.
If you don't care about people, you'll never understand their problems.
And if you don't understand their problems, you'll never earn their trust.

Whether dealing with a customer, a supplier, or a team member, I've found that *empathy* is the most powerful sales tool there is.
When someone feels you truly care about helping them — not about selling them — they listen, and they remember.

I've had team members tell me years later, *"I'll never forget when you believed in me, even when I doubted myself."*
That's leadership. That's sales. You're helping someone believe in their own potential.

Challenge for the Reader

This week, look for one situation where you need to "sell" something — an idea, a proposal, or a change.
Before you speak, stop and listen.
Ask yourself:

- What problem am I truly solving?
- How does this help the other person or the organization?
- Would I buy into this idea myself?

Then approach the conversation not as a salesperson, but as a **problem solver**.
If you can show others that your goal is to help them succeed, you won't need to convince them. They'll convince themselves.

Closing Reflection

Great leaders don't sell — they serve.
They don't push people — they inspire them to move.
They don't win arguments — they create understanding.
When your goal is to help others win, **success sells itself.**
And that's when sales, leadership, and integrity become the same thing.

Chapter 16. You Can't Lead Well on an Empty Tank
"A leader running on fumes leads others into the same fog."

I've seen it in factories, boardrooms, and construction sites — leaders running on fumes. Their eyes are tired, their patience is thin, and their decision-making is... well, let's just say it's not at its best.

And I'll be honest — I've been there too. For years, I thought the only way to prove my worth was to be the first one in and the last one out. To answer emails at midnight. To skip vacations because "the team needs me." It felt noble. Responsible. Even heroic. But in reality, I was slowly burning myself out — and when a leader burns out, the entire team feels it.

Leadership is not about how many hours you put in. It's about the quality of the hours you bring. And you can't bring quality if you're running on an empty tank.

The Lesson That Changed My Perspective

During my career, I've taken several personality profile assessments — DISC tests, in-depth trait evaluations — and they all painted a similar picture: I'm a very driven person, a natural implementer. I focus intensely on a task and work tirelessly until it's done.

That's exactly how I approached my first job as a cost engineer. I worked so many hours to meet deadlines that I barely had time to spend my earnings — everything was closed by the time I left the office.

One project in particular pushed me to the limit. I was tasked with optimizing how car seat patterns were arranged in a die to minimize material waste. It was like solving a giant jigsaw puzzle — first-row seats, second-row seats, sometimes third — moving, flipping, and rearranging them for the best yield. I became so absorbed in it that I started dreaming about the patterns at night. I couldn't sleep well, and the lack of rest eventually gave me headaches.

I noticed my department manager always looked fresh and well-rested, so one day, I asked him, "How do you manage to be so rested when you have more responsibilities than all of us?"

His answer stuck with me for life:

"I only worry about what I can control."

He asked me what was bothering me, so I told him about the die patterns and my work dreams. He listened and then said:

"Do you have the equipment to do that design work at home?"
"No," I replied.
"Then don't worry about it there. If you can finish it at the office, great — but if it's something that can't be done in one normal day, go home and get your mind on something else. Talk to your wife, your parents. Exercise — it's a great way to clear your mind. Or do a hobby you enjoy. What do you like?"
"I'm not much into sports, but I like music, photography, and traveling."
"There you go. Go home and do one of those things. On weekends, focus on activities that take work out of your mind and help you relax, so you come back Monday with fresh energy and maybe even new ideas."

It took me some time to follow that advice, but eventually, I did. And today, even writing this book — just like I did with The Road of a Dreamer — is part of how I continue to live out that lesson.

Leadership Insight:

"I only worry about what I can control." — This simple mindset shift can be the difference between burnout and balance.

Putting It into Practice

Years later, I had the chance to truly test that philosophy. My daughter was turning sixteen and chose to celebrate with a seven-day Caribbean cruise. I had the option to purchase Wi-Fi so I could stay connected to the rest of the world — and I made the decision not to. Not for me, not for any of us.

It turned out to be one of the best leadership decisions I ever made. We enjoyed those days together immensely — no work calls, no emails, no news updates. When I returned, the facility was still standing. My team leaders had made decisions in my absence — and most importantly, they had learned from them.

Sometimes as leaders, we feel out of place when we're not in control. But when you're not there, someone will carry the football to the finish line. Sure, I came back to thousands of emails and had to catch up. It took some extra work, but it was worth it. I returned full of energy, ready to tackle the temporary backlog, and I came back to a more mature team than the one I had left.

That trip became a cherished family memory, and it strengthened my conviction: you don't lose leadership by stepping away — you grow it.

Why Rest Is a Leadership Skill

Rest is not the opposite of work — it's part of the work. A leader who never recharges loses clarity, patience, and creativity. It's like driving a car with the check engine light on and hoping it will "just make it" to the next stop.

Some of my best ideas didn't come while sitting at my desk. They came while walking with my wife, cooking with my daughter, or watching the sunset with no phone in sight. Distance gives perspective.

Leading by Example

When leaders skip their vacation, the team notices. And even if you tell them to take their own time off, your actions send a louder message: "Time off is not really acceptable here."

If you truly want a healthy, sustainable culture, take your personal time — and encourage your people to do the same. Protect their right to recharge, because burned-out employees don't create innovation, they create turnover.

Practical Ways to Fill Your Tank

Plan downtime like you plan meetings. Put it on your calendar and guard it.
Truly disconnect. No "just checking emails." If you can't trust your team to handle things, you have a different problem to solve.
Find activities that restore you. For some it's travel, for others it's gardening, fishing, or playing an instrument. Whatever it is, make space for it.
Return with intention. When you come back, bring renewed focus, not a backlog of stress.

The Takeaway

You can't pour into your team if your own cup is empty. Taking time to recharge is not a luxury — it's a leadership responsibility. Because when you return rested, you bring your best self to the role, and your team deserves nothing less.

So, the next time you feel guilty about taking a break, remember: You're not stepping away from your leadership, you're stepping into it with more strength, clarity, and purpose.

Reader Reflection

As leaders, we often pride ourselves on our ability to push through, stay late, and "be there" for everyone else. But leadership is not a test of endurance — it's a balance of presence and preservation.

Take a moment to ask yourself:

When was the last time I took a true break — one where I fully disconnected from work?
What hobbies, activities, or relationships have I neglected because I've been "too busy"?
Do my actions show my team that rest is a part of performance, or that it's a luxury only taken when there's nothing left to do?
If I stepped away for a week, would my team be able to carry the football to the finish line without me? If not, what can I do to prepare them?

Challenge:

Plan one intentional period of downtime in the next 30 days — whether it's a weekend away, a hobby you enjoy, or simply an evening without emails. Use that time to recharge, and watch how your clarity, patience, and creativity improve when you return.

Remember: You can't lead well on an empty tank.

This chapter is about fueling yourself so you can show up at your best. Later in the book, we'll explore how resilience and balance extend beyond personal energy to the people and relationships who depend on you.

Leadership requires constant output, but you cannot give what you do not have. Protecting your health, your energy, and your ability to recover is not selfish — it is essential to serving others well. This chapter focuses on your personal energy and health — the fuel that makes leadership possible. Later, in Chapter 24, we'll explore how leaders must also look ahead to fuel the long-term health of their organizations, and in Chapter 25, how to protect the relationships and legacy that make the journey worthwhile.

Chapter 17. It's Only Business, Not Personal

"Leadership is personal—but decisions don't have to be emotional."

One of the toughest lessons I had to learn in leadership was that not every decision could be guided by friendship, sympathy, or loyalty. In the corporate world, results and responsibilities often weigh more than personal connections. That doesn't mean leaders should lose their humanity—it means they must carry the burden of decisions that affect both the business and the people who make it run.

The Pandemic Test

During the COVID pandemic, this reality became painfully clear. As customers slowed down and eventually shut their operations, we were forced to follow. One of our largest customers—an American automotive manufacturer—scaled back dramatically, and we had no choice but to mirror their actions. That meant sending people home.

These weren't just employees; they were men and women who had shown perfect attendance, who had supported the company with energy and commitment despite the uncertainty. They had families, bills, and obligations that weren't going to pause just because the world had. The hardest part was not knowing: no timeline for returning, no guarantees of who would come back, no way to answer the question that haunted me—Was this the last time I was going to see them?

As I mentioned in another chapter, layoffs are always among the hardest decisions a leader can face. But during COVID, the weight was unlike anything else I had experienced. Everyone understood the situation, but understanding doesn't make it easier. People still looked at their leaders for comfort and hope. The truth is, we as leaders were in the same situation, carrying the same questions with no answers.

I made it a point to stay in touch with some of them, to ask simply how they were doing. Those conversations, though small, created a sense of meaning in the middle of chaos. They reminded us we were not alone—that we were all fighting the same uncertainty together.

Ironically, months later, it was my turn to be laid off. After carrying the weight of sending others home, I too became part of the same story. And when operations eventually came back, I did not return to that tight, hardworking team I had once stood beside.

The Automation Dilemma

In another instance during my career, I was tested in a different way. As companies continue to compete globally, there is always pressure to deliver better results by reducing waste, improving utilization, and increasing efficiency. Earlier, I shared how global competitors pushed us to think differently and explore new technologies. Here, I want to describe the reality of what happens when that thinking leads to automation that directly displaces loyal workers.

The numbers were undeniable: automation would not only increase our bottom line, but more importantly, it was necessary to keep the business viable, competitive, and—most importantly—open. The decision was made—we would begin replacing several manual jobs with robots. On paper, our goal was to avoid losing jobs by retraining and moving employees into other areas. It sounded responsible, even compassionate. But reality is rarely that clean.

The truth was that most of the skills people had honed over years—sometimes decades—simply weren't transferable to the new operations. These were loyal workers who had built their identity, rhythm, and pride around their craft. And now, through no fault of their own, the very skills that once made them indispensable had become obsolete.

Conversations with the union were tense. We explained that if we didn't move in this direction, the entire organization could eventually disappear, taking everyone's jobs with it. It was a matter of survival. Yet that logic didn't make it easier to sit face-to-face with the very people who had given years of reliability and hard work and tell them their future had no room here.

We offered training, but not everyone could adapt. Some employees, through no fault of their own, simply couldn't learn or perform the new operations. The company became more efficient, more competitive—but the human cost was real. I knew we had done the right thing for the majority, but I also carried the bad feeling of knowing that good people had been left behind.

Suggestions for Leaders Facing Hard Decisions

Be Transparent and Honest – Don't sugarcoat or hide behind corporate jargon. People appreciate clarity, even if the message is painful.
Acknowledge the Human Cost – Recognize openly that the decision impacts lives. A few words of empathy can ease a heavy blow.
Communicate Early and Often – Silence breeds fear. Share updates, even when you don't have all the answers. It builds trust.
Offer Support Where Possible – Training, redeployment, or even just moral support matters. Even if all cannot be saved, some can be helped.
Involve People with Respect – Whether through union discussions or one-on-one talks, treat every individual with dignity.
Take Care of Yourself – These decisions weigh heavily. Leaders must also cope—by reflecting, seeking advice, and remembering that doing what's necessary doesn't mean you lack compassion.

Coping with the Weight of Leadership

For me, coping came from staying connected with people—sometimes just asking how they were doing. It reminded me that leadership is not about being untouchable but about sharing humanity in the middle of hard choices.

Another way was perspective: understanding that while some decisions bring immediate pain, they may secure survival for many others. Leaders must carry both truths at once, the survival of the organization and the sacrifice of individuals. It is a weight that never goes away, but one that defines what kind of leader you truly are.

Lesson Learned

My experience has always been in the manufacturing industry, where decisions about layoffs, automation, and restructuring directly affect people's lives. These are never easy, but they pale in comparison to the responsibilities carried by those in other professions—like a doctor telling a patient their cancer is at stage four, or a police officer knocking on a family's door to say their loved one is not coming home. Those are the hardest conversations anyone can have, and I cannot imagine the stress of carrying that weight day after day.

Sometimes we think people in those roles grow numb, that it becomes "just part of the job." But the truth is, no matter the industry, true leaders never become numb. They understand the impact of their words and decisions on people's lives, and they never lose sight of the human being on the other side of the conversation. That, to me, is the ultimate measure of leadership: to carry out difficult duties with fairness and courage, while never forgetting compassion.

In the end, it may be business, but it will always feel personal—and that's what makes us human.

Reader Reflection

Think about a time when you had to make—or witness—a difficult decision that affected others.
Did you focus only on the numbers, or did you also acknowledge the human side of that choice?
As leaders, we are often told to "separate business from emotion," but the truth is, our emotions are what make us capable of empathy and fairness. The key is not to remove emotion, it's to *manage* it with balance and integrity.

Reflect on how you communicate during times of uncertainty or change. Do people feel informed and respected, even when the news is difficult? Do they see compassion in your leadership, or only the execution of a directive?
True strength comes from carrying responsibility without losing humanity. The best leaders don't hide from the weight—they carry it with grace, honesty, and care.

Challenge for the Reader

In the next month, focus on **leading with transparency and compassion**, especially during hard conversations.

1. **Identify one difficult message** you've been avoiding—whether it's a tough performance discussion, a project setback, or a change in direction. Plan how to communicate it with honesty and empathy.
2. **Acknowledge the human impact.** Before delivering the message, take a moment to imagine how the other person will feel. Adjust your approach to show understanding, not just authority.

3. **Stay connected after the decision.** Follow up. Ask how they're doing and what support they might need to move forward.
4. **Reflect afterward.** Write down what went well and what could have been handled differently. This practice builds your emotional intelligence and prepares you for future challenges.

Leadership is not measured by how well we handle success, it's defined by how we lead through loss, change, and uncertainty. The next time you face a difficult decision, remember: it may be business, but it will always be personal. Lead as if both matter, because they do.

Chapter 18. Partnering with Human Resources — Leading People, Not Just Processes

"HR becomes powerful the moment leaders stop treating it as a formality."

A Second Set of Eyes

I have always believed that every leader needs a second set of eyes—someone to ask the questions you might not have asked yourself. For me, one of the departments I have always worked very closely with is Human Resources. Over the years, I've had the privilege of learning from excellent managers like Shannon, Aubrey, and others, who taught me a simple but powerful truth: there are always at least two perspectives to consider when making decisions that impact a person.

How you handle a situation can make all the difference. The right approach can inspire someone to grow into a better employee, while a careless word can turn them into an upset person whose professional future in the company becomes clouded. I have always believed that it is not only the message you convey, but the way you deliver it that truly matters.

The Engineer's Mindset vs. The Human Factor

My background is in Industrial Engineering, which means my natural instinct is to optimize processes, set up standards, improve layouts, reduce wasted motion, and eliminate inefficiencies. It's easier when the focus is on machines, materials, or the environment—things you can measure, design, and predict.

But people are not machines. There is no blueprint, no standard pattern, no fixed rule for how each person will react. Unlike equipment, people bring with them unique physical, emotional, and cultural identities. Some are taller, younger, more experienced, or come from different backgrounds with very different expectations. You cannot assume that one rule will apply to all.

The employee handbook may outline the same expectations for everyone, but the way you approach each individual must be adapted. To motivate one person may require encouragement; to correct another may require firmness. HR has always helped me see those nuances, reminding me that leadership is not about applying a single standard but about finding the right approach for each person while keeping fairness and consistency at the center.

A Hard First Lesson in Leadership

During my younger years, as I began to take on the responsibility of leading people, I faced one of the hardest tasks any leader can encounter: letting a team member go.

Without going into all the details, this individual had made a decision that could not simply be overlooked or reduced to a lesser penalty, like a final written warning. After gathering all the evidence, I shared it with the Human Resources Manager. He reviewed everything carefully, and the justification was clear. The employee had violated one of the company's principal expectations, something so serious that termination was the only possible outcome.

The decision was made. Now the responsibility was mine. I had to be the one to deliver the news. I was given a folder containing the termination letter and supporting documents. Armed with those papers, I thought I was prepared. In reality, I was not.

It was early in the morning, around 9:00 a.m., when I called the engineer into my cubicle. My space had half walls and large glass panes—it offered some privacy, but not complete separation from the rest of the team. I closed the door, asked him to sit, and explained the situation step by step. This was not a surprise to him. He knew I had witnessed the incident, and he knew I had reported it to HR. Up to that point, everything was calm and professional.

But when I told him the decision was to let him go, his reaction was something I had never anticipated. He broke down crying, fell to his knees, and grabbed my legs, pleading with me not to fire him. He begged, promising he would never repeat the mistake, that he needed the job, that I should reconsider.

As this unfolded, I looked up and saw my entire team of engineers watching through the glass—standing silently, staring at the scene. To them, without context, it must have looked shocking and humiliating: their coworker on his knees, crying, clinging to me, while I stood frozen.

I asked him several times to please stand up. I told him I understood this was painful but reminded him of the seriousness of what he had done. Still, he refused. With all eyes on me, I finally had no choice but to call security. They entered, took him by the arms, and escorted him out of the building. The silence afterward was heavy.

The impact on the rest of the team was immediate. For days, no one spoke to me. Their eyes carried judgment and resentment. Because of confidentiality, I could not explain the details of what had happened. They were left to imagine, and in their minds, I became the villain—the boss who had humiliated and discarded one of their peers.

When I debriefed with HR afterward, they reassured me I had followed the right process. But they also gave me advice that stayed with me: it's not just about the decision itself, it's about how, where, and when you deliver it. The environment matters. The preparation matters. The way you anticipate reactions and plan your approach matters.

That experience taught me a lesson I've carried ever since. I now never go into these conversations without discussing not only the issue at hand and the resolution with HR, but also the *setting* and the possible scenarios. I try to visualize Plan A, Plan B, and Plan C:

- What if the person reacts calmly?
- What if they get angry or even violent?
- What if they break down emotionally?

Each of these requires a different response, and part of leadership is being prepared for all of them.

From that day forward, I understood that while HR provides the framework, the leader's responsibility is to deliver with humanity, foresight, and respect. Processes can be followed, but people react in unpredictable ways—and how you handle that moment shapes not only the individual leaving but also the trust of everyone who stays.

Key Areas Where Leaders and HR Must Align

1. **Hiring and Retention**
   A great hire can transform a team. A poor one can poison culture for years. Leaders must work hand in hand with HR to define what kind of people they want to bring in, not only in terms of skills but in terms of values, teamwork, and long-term potential.
2. **Training and Development**
   Machines break down without maintenance; people stagnate without growth. HR can be a key ally in creating programs for leadership development, technical training, and cross-training—ensuring people feel invested in and prepared for future opportunities.
3. **Conflict Resolution**
   Ignoring conflict does not make it disappear; it makes it worse.

Partnering with HR gives leaders the tools and neutral perspective to address problems fairly and consistently, avoiding favoritism and protecting culture.

4. **Employee Engagement**
   Recognition programs, career paths, surveys, and open communication channels often originate with HR, but they only work when leaders actively support them. HR may design the framework, but leaders give it life.
5. **Policy as a Framework, Not a Cage**
   HR policies are often seen as restrictions. In reality, they provide structure to ensure fairness and consistency. Strong leaders know how to apply them with wisdom and empathy—guidelines, not chains.

Lessons Learned

- HR is not an administrative department—it's a leadership ally.
- Processes don't run without people; and people don't thrive without fair policies, growth opportunities, and recognition.
- Partnering with HR is not optional; it's essential for sustainable leadership.
- Treat policies as tools for fairness, not obstacles to flexibility.
- Leading people well means working with HR to balance business needs and human needs.

Reader Reflection

Leadership isn't only about making the right decision — it's about delivering it the right way.

Ask yourself:

- Do I see HR as an ally in leadership decisions, or just as an administrative function?

- Before delivering difficult news, do I prepare for different possible reactions — calm, angry, or emotional?
- How much thought do I give to the *setting* and *tone* of the message, not just the content?
- Am I balancing fairness and consistency with empathy and respect when handling sensitive issues?

Challenge:

Before your next difficult conversation, sit down with HR and walk through three possible scenarios:

1. The person accepts the decision calmly.
2. The person gets angry or defensive.
3. The person becomes emotional or distressed.

Prepare how you will respond in each case. The more prepared you are, the more confidence and humanity you'll project — and the more trust you'll preserve with your team.

Chapter 19. Industrial and Process Engineering: Designing Systems for People and Performance

"A process that ignores people is a process built to fail."

My profession is Industrial Engineering — the career I chose and the one I loved so much that I graduated twice: first in Mexico, from the Universidad Autónoma del Noreste in Saltillo, Coahuila, and later, after moving to the United States, from New Mexico State University.

From the beginning, I realized that Industrial Engineering is different from most other engineering disciplines. While mechanical, electrical, or civil engineers dive deep into a single specialty, Industrial Engineers are trained to see across disciplines. It is not about going narrow and deep into one subject, but about combining knowledge from many fields to analyze, improve, and integrate processes.

That versatility is what makes the field so powerful. Industrial Engineering can be applied almost anywhere — in banks, hospitals, airports, service industries, or manufacturing. We learn a little about everything, which allows us to understand the bigger picture and not just a single component.

The way I see it, Industrial Engineering is about designing systems of processes that work together to achieve a specific result — and once that result is established, ensuring the system is standardized, maintained, and continuously improved.

With this mindset, I've had the privilege to work across many areas of organizations: engineering, maintenance, production, sales, and supply chain. No matter the department, there is always a system to analyze, optimize, and align with performance goals. That's the gift of Industrial Engineering — it teaches us to look at organizations as living systems.

Tools That Shape Systems and Performance

Throughout my career, I've relied on specific Industrial Engineering tools that have consistently improved performance while respecting people. Some of the most impactful include:

- **Lean Manufacturing & Kaizen** – A philosophy of eliminating waste (time, motion, inventory, defects) and creating value through continuous improvement. I've seen small Kaizen events transform entire workflows and boost morale because people see their ideas put into practice.
- **Six Sigma & Statistical Process Control (SPC)** – Methods for reducing variation, improving quality, and solving chronic process issues using data. These tools shift the conversation from opinions to facts, which strengthens trust between leaders and teams.
- **Value Stream Mapping (VSM)** – A visual way to see the flow of materials and information, identifying bottlenecks and inefficiencies. It's like shining a flashlight into the dark corners of a process where waste hides.
- **Time Studies & Work Sampling** – Observing and measuring how tasks are performed. This is not about rushing people but about uncovering unnecessary steps, poor layouts, or outdated methods that frustrate employees.
- **Simulation and Modeling** – Using software to model processes and test "what if" scenarios before making costly changes. I've used this in plant layouts and logistics flows to save both money and time.
- **5S and Visual Management** – Organizing the workplace so that "what is normal" is clear to everyone. When systems are visible, problems become obvious, and solutions are easier to implement.

Each of these tools has something in common: they are not just about numbers or efficiency. They are about creating **systems that work for people** — systems that reduce stress, eliminate guesswork, and free employees to focus on value-adding work.

Leadership Through Systems Thinking

Industrial Engineering isn't just about charts and graphs; it's about leadership. When leaders adopt a systems mindset, they stop blaming individuals for failures and start asking: *What in the system caused this result?*

For example, if an operator makes repeated mistakes, is it because they are careless, or because the process wasn't clearly defined? If deliveries are consistently late, is it because of lazy employees, or because the system of scheduling, purchasing, and logistics is broken?

Leaders who think like Industrial Engineers design systems that:

- Support employees instead of setting them up for failure.
- Reward the right behaviors, not just the fastest output.
- Encourage innovation by showing that processes can evolve.

This mindset shifts responsibility from individuals alone to the leaders who design the environment. A well-designed system becomes a quiet form of leadership — guiding behavior, driving performance, and showing people what "good" looks like.

Lessons Learned

- Industrial Engineers are system designers — our role is to see the big picture and align processes for performance and people.
- The best systems are not rigid; they are adaptable, allowing improvement and innovation.

- Tools like Lean, Six Sigma, and VSM are powerful, but they only work if leaders respect the people running the process.
- Leadership is about owning the system — and continuously improving it so that everyone can succeed.

Key Tools of Industrial and Process Engineering

While Industrial Engineering offers many methods, I've found a core set of tools that consistently deliver results across industries. These tools not only improve performance but also simplify work and support the people who make systems succeed. The table below summarizes the most practical ones I've used throughout my career:

Tool	Purpose	Example Use
Lean & Kaizen	Eliminate waste and drive continuous improvement.	Conducting a Kaizen event to reduce changeover time on a press line.
Six Sigma & SPC	Reduce variation and improve quality using data.	Using SPC charts to monitor scrap trends and prevent defects.
Value Stream Mapping (VSM)	Visualize the flow of materials and information to find bottlenecks.	Mapping the order-to-delivery process to reduce lead time.
Time Studies & Work Sampling	Measure work methods and identify inefficiencies.	Studying assembly line tasks to balance workloads across stations.

Tool	Purpose	Example Use
Simulation & Modeling	Test process changes before implementation.	Using software to model a new plant layout for material flow.
5S & Visual Management	Organize the workplace to make problems visible.	Implementing color-coded zones and tool boards to improve discipline.

Closing Paragraph

At the end of the day, tools are only as good as the leaders who apply them. Lean, Six Sigma, or simulation models can transform a process, but if they are used without respect for people, they become nothing more than pressure tactics. The true power of Industrial Engineering lies in designing systems that help people succeed — systems that make work safer, clearer, and more meaningful. When leaders apply these tools with purpose and respect, they don't just improve performance; they create environments where people can thrive.

Reader Reflection

In your current role, do you focus more on individual performance or on the system that shapes it?

Where are the hidden inefficiencies or frustrations in your workplace — and what tools could you use to uncover them?

As a leader, how can you design processes that respect people while still driving performance?

Challenge: Map and Improve One System

Choose one system in your workplace — it could be how you start meetings, process orders, schedule maintenance, or manage inventory.

Map It — Draw the flow from start to finish, showing each step, handoff, or decision point.

Identify Waste — Look for unnecessary steps, delays, rework, or confusion. Ask: *Where are people getting frustrated?*

Apply One Tool — Use a simple Industrial Engineering method (5S, Value Stream Mapping, or a Time Study) to uncover opportunities for improvement.

Take Action — Implement at least one improvement and measure the result. Did it reduce time, cost, or frustration?

The goal isn't perfection. The challenge is to practice seeing systems as an Industrial Engineer would — as interconnected processes that can be simplified, standardized, and improved for both people and performance.

Chapter 20. New Technologies to Simplify and Eliminate
"Technology should remove complexity—not create dependence."

Introduction

Technology has always promised to make work easier—but too often, it complicates instead of simplifies. In a world where global competitors combine low-cost labor with state-of-the-art automation, the real question is not what can this new tool do? but what can it eliminate? In this chapter, we explore how leaders can harness technology to simplify processes, eliminate waste, and stay competitive in an increasingly automated world—while also preparing for the next wave of innovation with AI, VR, and advanced simulations.

Competition as the Driver of Innovation

I have always believed that the biggest source of innovation is competition—and today, competition is global. If we want to remain a viable option for customers, we must continuously challenge ourselves not only on quality and on-time delivery, but most importantly on cost.

For years, I heard conversations like: "They are taking all the business overseas because their labor is cheaper." And yes, in some cases that is true, especially with hourly personnel. The cost of living in the United States cannot be compared to countries like Mexico, India, or Taiwan. But that assumption only tells part of the story.

When I invited colleagues to travel with me and actually see those operations abroad, they were often surprised. Many carried a preconceived image: that they would find dirty, dark factories with workers exposed to unsafe conditions, poor quality standards, and little regulation—but all of it justified by "cheap labor."

What they found instead was a shock. The reality wasn't just cheaper labor. In many cases, it was less labor—because entire processes had already been replaced by automation, robotics, and smarter technologies. Those companies were running state-of-the-art facilities, often cleaner, safer, and more advanced than what we were using at home. This quick shock to their beliefs opened their eyes to a truth: we weren't losing business only because of low wages. We were losing because we had failed to innovate.

The Trap of Complexity

But technology alone does not guarantee success. The very tools designed to help us can also complicate our work if used carelessly. A new ERP system, a scheduling tool, or an advanced sensor network might be introduced with the promise of efficiency. Yet, if not carefully applied, they generate new layers of confusion, endless data entry, or multiple dashboards nobody looks at.

True leadership is not about introducing technology for its own sake it's about simplifying and eliminating waste.

Technology as a Simplifier

The most powerful technologies are not the ones that do more, but the ones that allow you to do less.

Automation eliminates repetitive tasks.

Integration replaces double entry across systems.

Dashboards that highlight only the few KPIs that matter save hours of chasing numbers.

Predictive maintenance eliminates firefighting by addressing failures before they happen.

Each of these examples turns complexity into clarity. The test for any new technology is simple: Does it remove steps, decisions, or confusion?

Elimination Before Addition

Leaders must resist the temptation to pile on technology without discipline. The first question should not be What can this system do? but rather What can this system eliminate?

For example:

A new inspection system should eliminate manual logs, not just digitize them.
A new planning software should eliminate redundant meetings, not create more reports.
A new HR platform should eliminate paperwork, not generate longer onboarding forms.

Lessons from the Shop Floor

I have witnessed plants adopt complex scheduling tools that took weeks of training—yet a simple whiteboard and clear shift ownership delivered better results. Conversely, I've seen predictive monitoring systems revolutionize maintenance by preventing failures that once cost millions.

The lesson is not about rejecting or embracing technology. It is about applying it with surgical precision: choose tools that simplify, and eliminate what no longer adds value.

Emerging Tools for the Future

There are also new technologies emerging that will reshape how we work and lead. Artificial Intelligence can already analyze vast amounts of data and provide options to guide better decision-making. Virtual Reality may soon allow frontline workers to solve problems using real-time manuals displayed through their lenses. Simulations can help us foresee potential failures before they happen, preparing us with solutions in advance.

Some of these tools are still developing, but they will only grow more robust in the years ahead. As leaders, we cannot afford to ignore them. We must begin to embrace these technologies and learn how to apply them to our jobs. Because while we hesitate, others around the world are already asking the same questions, experimenting with the same tools, and racing ahead.

The key is to be open to change—to explore how these technologies can simplify, eliminate waste, and strengthen our competitiveness. As leaders, it is our responsibility not only to adopt these tools, but to guide our teams in using them to sustain and grow our businesses in the face of global competition.

Lessons Learned

Competition is the strongest driver of innovation—and it is now global.
Low-cost labor is only part of the story; technology adoption often matters more.
The purpose of technology is not to add complexity, but to simplify and eliminate waste.
Before adopting a new tool, ask what it will remove, not just what it can add.

Emerging technologies like AI, VR, and simulations must be embraced early, or others will pass us by.

Leaders must set the tone be open to change, guide your teams, and ensure technology serves people—not the other way around.

Reader Reflection

What technologies in your workplace are truly simplifying, and which are complicating?

Where are you relying on "cheap labor" assumptions instead of exploring smarter automation?

If you had to eliminate one outdated process or system tomorrow, what would it be?

How can you begin learning about AI, VR, or simulation tools today—before your competitors do?

Challenge for the Reader

Over the next 30 days, take a close look at how technology is used in your area of responsibility—not to admire it, but to question it.

1. **Identify one process that creates more work than value.** Ask yourself: "Is this tool simplifying or complicating?" If it's adding steps, find a way to eliminate or streamline it.
2. **Engage your team in a discussion** about what technologies actually help them versus those that slow them down. Collect their feedback honestly—often the people closest to the process know exactly where inefficiencies hide.
3. **Select one improvement opportunity** and build a small test. Try simplifying it with automation, integration, or elimination. Measure the result and share what you learn.
4. **Explore an emerging technology.** Spend at least one hour learning about AI, VR, or predictive analytics—how they apply

to your industry, and what small step your team could take to experiment with them.

Remember: **the goal of technology is not to impress—it's to improve.**
Leaders who master simplicity build organizations that move faster, think smarter, and stay ahead of change. Start today by eliminating one unnecessary step—and you'll be one step closer to true innovation.

Chapter 21. Traps and Mistakes Leaders Can Commit
"Most leadership mistakes grow from what we refuse to see."

Introduction: The Hidden Pitfalls of Leadership

Leadership is not just about setting vision and driving results, it's also about avoiding the subtle traps that can quietly undermine trust, morale, and long-term success. Many leaders stumble not because they lack intelligence or ambition, but because they fall into patterns of behavior that seem harmless at first yet grow into obstacles for themselves and their teams. Recognizing these traps early is critical.

Most leaders share some common traits. They are relentless. They are fearless. They make the hard decisions others avoid. They carry self-confidence and know how to engage people toward ideas and goals. Because of this, people naturally look up to them—expecting strength, direction, and certainty, even in the face of the toughest calls.

But admiration comes with shadows. What some see as inspiration, others may perceive as arrogance, favoritism, or detachment. As leaders conquer problems and accumulate success, admiration mixes with envy, respect with resentment, and confidence with expectation. Pressure builds—not only to perform at work but to project an image of control in every area of life. This is where the cracks often begin to show.

Common Traps Leaders Fall Into

1. Believing You Must Have All the Answers
A leader who tries to answer every question and solve every problem personally may appear strong, but in reality, this stifles initiative and prevents the team from growing. The trap is equating leadership with omniscience rather than guidance.

2. Favoritism and Inequity

Treating certain employees with more leniency, praise, or opportunities quickly erodes trust. Even small signs of favoritism create division, resentment, and disengagement.

3. Confusing Activity with Results

Filling calendars with endless meetings, checklists, or reports may look productive, but unless those activities drive results, they are distractions. Leaders must constantly ask: "Is this moving the organization forward?"

4. Ignoring Frontline Voices

Many leaders unintentionally distance themselves from the shop floor, customer service desk, or sales calls. Without feedback from the people closest to the problems, leaders risk blind spots that lead to poor decisions.

5. Avoiding Hard Conversations

Some leaders fall into the trap of avoiding conflict to keep peace. Yet, not addressing poor performance, toxic behavior, or broken processes is one of the fastest ways to lose credibility.

6. Micromanaging

Trust is broken when leaders insist on controlling every detail. Micromanagement drains creativity, frustrates high performers, and leaves the leader overworked and exhausted.

7. Becoming a Victim of Success

Leaders who achieve early wins may become complacent or overconfident. What worked yesterday won't necessarily work tomorrow. The trap is failing to keep learning, adapting, and improving.

8. Unhealthy Coping With Pressure

As leaders climb higher, the weight of responsibility can become overwhelming. The expectation isn't just to deliver results, it's to appear unshakable in every situation. This illusion of invulnerability pushes some leaders toward unhealthy escapes: alcohol, drugs, risky relationships, or other forms of self-destruction.

At first, these habits may feel like "relief" or a way to keep going. But over time, they erode credibility, harm relationships, and can undo years of leadership. Every vessel has its limit; pressure must find an outlet. If the outlet is destructive, the damage is inevitable.

A Cautionary Tale: Coping Through Escape

Early in my career, I worked closely with a senior leader who carried the weight of enormous responsibility. To cope, he sometimes turned to unhealthy outlets—late nights, alcohol, anything to escape the pressure. He had vision, drive, and the ability to rally people around a goal. When he visited our facility, we pushed ourselves to new levels of performance. But at the end of those long days, he often suggested dinner and drinks.

One drink became two, then three, until the night spiraled out of control. It wasn't about celebration—it was about escape. He was carrying the enormous weight of responsibility and chose alcohol as his release valve. I often found myself quietly taking care of him, making sure he got back safely and wasn't embarrassed in front of others.

That experience taught me a lasting lesson: leaders are human, and their strength hides real vulnerability. What most people saw was a confident mentor; what I saw was a man buckling under invisible pressure.

I don't condone such behavior, but I understand it. Pressure, if not managed in healthy ways, will always find an outlet.

Another Cautionary Tale: When Professional Becomes Personal

On another occasion, I was sitting at home in the United States when I received a call from Mexico. One of the ladies on my team was very upset, and the conversation went something like this:

"Hello, Héctor, I am calling you because I am very upset and I am tired of this situation. The assistant of the Vice President keeps on messing with me, and I've had it. I am just calling to complain and also to tell you I am going to speak with her, and I don't know how this will turn out, but I am done with this situation."

I asked her to calm down and explain what was making her so upset. She said, "She keeps on messing with my things. Yesterday she removed my name from my desk. Today she put my name backwards on the check-in board. These may seem small, but it's happening every day and I'm tired of it."

To me, these seemed like small details pointing to a deeper issue. I knew some background: this woman had been the Vice President's assistant for years, traveling with him and managing his schedule. Eventually, he reassigned her and hired a new assistant who had less experience. Both felt threatened, and their rivalry spilled into the workplace. Both women felt threatened by the other, and their rivalry spilled into the workplace.

With this in mind, I asked her not to confront the new assistant directly. Doing so could escalate into a fight that might cost one or both of them their jobs—and both were valuable to the company. She calmed down, and I promised to address it.

After hanging up, I called the Vice President. I explained the issue and reminded him that, knowingly or unknowingly, he had created this situation. Now he needed to solve it. I advised him to meet with both assistants, clearly define their roles, and insist that their relationship remain professional—or face consequences.

After that, things improved. They still didn't like each other, but at least they became professional and cordial inside the workplace.

This was a vivid reminder that leaders can sometimes create traps themselves. When boundaries blur, when relationships are perceived as personal instead of professional, it breeds jealousy, division, and conflict. Even seemingly small issues can spiral into bigger problems if not addressed with clarity and firmness.

Lessons Learned

Self-awareness is protection. Regularly ask: What trap might I be falling into right now?
Feedback is a mirror. Encourage your team, mentors, and peers to call out blind spots.
Courage matters. Avoiding hard conversations today creates bigger problems tomorrow.
Balance is key. Delegate without disconnecting, monitor without micromanaging, lead without favoritism.
Manage stress before it manages you. Build healthy outlet exercise, reflection, mentoring, or family time.
Guard boundaries. Professional admiration can sometimes blur dependency or inappropriate closeness.

Reflection for the Reader

Which of these traps do you recognize in yourself or your workplace?
How do you react when someone points out a blind spot?

What safeguards can you put in place to prevent these traps from becoming habits?

How do you cope with pressure—and are those coping mechanisms healthy or destructive?

"The higher you rise, the more vital it becomes to guard against the mistakes that can bring you down."

Challenge for the Reader

In the coming weeks, take a proactive step to identify and address one potential leadership trap before it becomes a habit.

1. Pick one trap from this chapter that resonates most with you—whether it's micromanagement, avoiding conflict, favoritism, or unhealthy coping with stress. Be honest with yourself.
2. Ask for perspective. Choose one trusted peer, mentor, or team member and ask for candid feedback: *"Do you ever see me falling into this pattern?"* Listen without defensiveness.
3. Create one safeguard. This could be a simple rule—delegating one decision each week, setting limits on work hours, or committing to have hard conversations within 48 hours of recognizing an issue.
4. Track your progress for 30 days. Reflect weekly on moments when you caught yourself slipping and how you corrected course.
5. Share your learning. Use your experience to help another leader or colleague avoid the same trap.

Remember, leadership excellence doesn't come from perfection—it comes from awareness, humility, and the courage to grow. When you commit to confronting your own blind spots, you not only protect your credibility—you also strengthen the trust and respect of everyone who follows you.

Closing Bridge

Leadership is as much about avoiding mistakes as it is about building strengths. The traps we've explored are cautionary markers, reminding us that leadership carries both privilege and danger. The question is not whether you will face these temptations, it's how you will respond when they appear.

And one of the most powerful tools to help leaders avoid these traps is communication and feedback. Clear, open dialogue keeps leaders grounded, exposes blind spots, and offers healthier ways to handle pressure. In the next chapter, we will explore how feedback—given and received—can transform a leader's growth, strengthen relationships, and become a compass that keeps us from drifting into these very mistakes.

Chapter 22. Leading Through Change and Conflict

"Change is hard because it forces us to choose between comfort and progress."

The Pressure of Change

One of the most challenging aspects of my career has been working in startups and turnaround situations. These environments are exciting, but they also push people to their limits. Stress levels rise, uncertainty grows, and not everyone knows how to react. Left unmanaged, this stress can create bigger problems than the ones we are trying to solve.

Over the years, I've come to believe there are two main types of people: those who thrive on the excitement and adrenaline of solving problems, and those who excel at maintaining stability once systems are running smoothly. Both roles are essential—but they are rarely found in the same person.

When launching a new facility, this tension becomes obvious. The startup team focuses on getting the building ready, equipment installed, and services running. But those people aren't usually the ones who will operate the machines. That gap—between **theory and practice**—can spark conflict and resistance.

The Mold Line Lesson

I remember when we installed a new molding line. On paper, the equipment was designed to run at 120 molds per hour. It looked great in theory but reaching that speed wasn't just about engineering—it was about culture and expectations.

We brought in a molding supervisor with years of experience. The challenge on this line was not the machine itself but the manual step: two operators had to insert cores by hand into each mold.

When I first spoke to the supervisor, I asked him to push the line to its maximum speed. "Don't worry if the operators can't keep up," I told him. "Some molds will go empty, and that's fine. We won't pour metal into them, and we'll recycle the sand. What matters is that they get used to the speed of the line."

That first day, I timed it, the line was running at 120 molds per hour.

The next morning, it was down to 60. When I asked why, the supervisor said, "Because the operators can't keep up." I reminded him of our plan: the goal was to set expectations from the beginning. If we allowed the team to settle at half speed, every future attempt to increase it would feel like an unfair demand.

He agreed and put it back at 120.

The following day, I found it slowed again. This time, he told me, "I was brought here for my years of experience. I know what I am doing." I acknowledged his expertise but explained something just as important: *I knew the culture.* If expectations weren't set early, every change would become a fight.

On the third day, the story repeated. I gave him an ultimatum:

"This line was designed and quoted to run at 120 molds per hour. If we don't run at that speed, our costs will exceed what we promised our customers. That will create financial problems. If the line is not at 120 by next week, I will have to let you go, and I will personally train the personnel."

Nothing changed. I spoke with the owner and released him from his job.

I then met with the operators directly. I told them I didn't expect perfection right away, only their best effort. I explained why the speed mattered: if we didn't run at 120 molds per hour, our costs would rise and we could lose business.

To my surprise, they embraced it. Within a month, they were consistently running at speed. Even though some molds went empty at first, they adapted. Complaints disappeared. The expectation had become the standard.

Leadership Highlights from the Mold Line

- **Set expectations from day one.** Habits formed early are difficult to change later.
- **Explain the "why."** People are more willing to stretch when they understand the bigger picture.
- **Don't compromise with underperformance.** Temporary comfort can create permanent resistance.

When Personal Ties Create Resistance

Not all conflicts are technical. Some are deeply personal. Another challenge I've faced is when multiple family members or friends work at the same company. Loyalty within these groups can create distortions. People share only their side of a story with those closest to them, and soon rumors become more powerful than facts.

In one company, sales were dipping, and the decline put heavy strain on operations. The less work we had, the more difficult decisions I had to make in production. These weren't performance-based terminations, we were losing good people simply because there wasn't enough work to keep them productive.

I developed a way to track our backlog and forecast. What I saw alarmed me: new products weren't replacing the old ones being phased out. We were facing a dangerous gap.

In meetings, the sales manager constantly blamed other departments, quality, production, engineering. I recognized this as a deflection. The real problem was clear: we weren't bringing in new customers.

The owner asked me to take a closer look at the sales department. What I found confirmed my suspicion. Instead of seeking new opportunities, the focus was on waiting for existing customers to send more work. That's not growth, that's slow decline.

I tried working with the sales manager, but it quickly became clear that he lacked the drive and skills to develop new business. I stepped in myself, reaching out to former contacts and beginning the long process of building relationships. These conversations can take years before they bear fruit—most suppliers are locked into three-to-five-year cycles unless their current vendor fails badly.

As I pushed harder, the sales manager didn't see accountability as a challenge. He saw it as a threat. Rather than adapt, he turned to his network of friends inside the company, many of whom were related to one another. He spread stories about me—some exaggerated, some outright false. Soon, rumors circulated about what a "bad manager" I was.

Eventually, I had to act. I let him go. One of his closest friends quit in protest. Others stayed but continued to spread gossip. Some even carried their negativity into exit interviews when they eventually left for other jobs.

I could have spent my energy chasing down every rumor. Instead, I focused on the mission: bringing in new business. Slowly, the conversations I had started months before turned into small orders, and eventually into larger quotes. The turnaround began, even as negativity lingered in the background.

Leadership Highlights from the Sales Conflict

- **Focus on results, not rumors.** Let your work and outcomes do the talking.
- **Separate personal ties from professional accountability.** Friendship cannot replace performance.
- **Don't get trapped in deflections.** Keep redirecting conversations back to the real problem.
- **Accept that not everyone will like you.** Leadership requires resilience against criticism.

Lessons in Leading Through Conflict

These two stories—one about machines, the other about people—taught me lasting lessons about leadership during change and conflict:

- **Set expectations early.** The longer you allow lower standards, the harder it becomes to raise them.
- **Culture trumps theory.** Expertise matters, but so does knowing how people think, act, and resist.
- **Conflict is inevitable.** Whether it's technical resistance or personal rumors, leaders must face it directly.
- **Not everyone will like you.** Leadership is not about pleasing everyone—it's about securing the future of the business.
- **Stay focused on the mission.** Rumors, resistance, and setbacks are distractions. The leader's job is to keep the organization moving forward.

A Challenge for You

Think about a change or conflict you are facing right now. It might be technical, cultural, or personal. Ask yourself:

1. **What expectation have I set—or failed to set—that could be creating resistance?**
2. **Am I spending more energy fighting rumors and excuses, or focusing on results?**
3. **If I had to act decisively tomorrow, what would that look like?**

Your challenge is to pick **one situation** where conflict has been holding you back and apply these lessons. Don't wait for perfect conditions—set the expectation, explain the "why," and act with clarity.

Conclusion: Turning Turbulence Into Trust

Change will always create conflict. Some conflicts come from machines that won't run the way they should. Others come from people who resist accountability. In both cases, the role of a leader is not to avoid the storm but to steer through it with clarity and conviction.

In the end, leadership is about turning fear into focus, resistance into resilience, and turbulence into trust. The goal is not to win popularity contests, it's to secure the future, for the business and for the people who depend on it.

Key Takeaways

- **Set expectations early.** People adapt faster when the standard is clear from the beginning.
- **Explain the "why."** Understanding the bigger picture reduces resistance.

- **Culture trumps theory.** Expertise must be balanced with cultural alignment.
- **Focus on results, not rumors.** Let outcomes speak louder than opinions.
- **Don't compromise with underperformance.** Temporary comfort creates long-term struggle.
- **Separate personal ties from accountability.** Friendship can't replace performance.
- **Stay focused on the mission.** Distractions are inevitable; your role is to keep moving forward.
- **Accept that not everyone will like you.** Leadership requires resilience and conviction.

Chapter 23. Mentoring and Developing Others
"Mentoring is not teaching—it's unlocking."

The Hidden Responsibility of Leadership

One of the greatest responsibilities of leadership is not simply achieving results but ensuring that others are prepared to carry the torch after you. Too often, leaders focus on immediate outcomes—production numbers, quarterly goals, profitability—and forget that the true measure of their legacy is found in the people they influenced, taught, and helped grow.

When I look back at my career, the most meaningful accomplishments were not only tied to machines that ran better, or plants that exceeded expectations, but to the people who became stronger leaders under my watch. Mentorship is about multiplying leadership. It is about taking what you've learned through trials, mistakes, and victories, and passing it forward.

A Mentor Who Taught Me How to Fish

Early in my career, I found a great mentor. The reason I consider him a mentor is not because he gave me solutions, but because he challenged me to find them myself. A typical example of not giving me the fish but teaching me how to fish.

I remember one quotation I was preparing in 1993. There was no production volume listed for a particular project, but I knew it was for a vehicle, I knew the brand, and I was certain the information had to exist somewhere. This was before the internet was a tool at our fingertips—there was no Google, no ChatGPT, nothing you could just type into and instantly find an answer.

So I approached an engineer named Ken. He had been with the company for more than 20 years. At first glance, Ken seemed rough, always upset about something—but later I learned that was simply his personality. I asked him, *"Based on your experience quoting different car platforms, do you know what volume I should use for this component?"*

Ken looked at me and said:

"Well, I can tell you, but then you won't learn anything. And how can you even trust what I tell you? Your name will be on that quote—you want to be sure, don't you?"

I replied, *"Yes, I don't want to make a mistake, but I trust you would give me the right answer."*

He shook his head. *"That's the wrong answer. I can make mistakes too. So instead, let me show you how to find the information."*

Ken pulled out a book I had never seen before. He explained that the automotive industry is very planning-driven. Companies know the production rate of each line and plan production days for the entire year. Together, we researched where the car was being manufactured and found the two locations. Then we looked up the planned daily production rates, multiplied by the 250 production days scheduled that year, and adjusted for the different model mixes—base models, high-end versions, service models, and so on.

By the end of the exercise, we had estimated the total volume for the vehicle platform. The calculations gave me confidence in the number I used for the quote. Later, I learned that our assumptions were spot on.

But the real lesson wasn't just the process. It was the realization that when someone shares knowledge and guidance—not just answers—it helps others grow. Ken could have given me a number and walked away. Instead, he challenged me, and in doing so, he taught me how to think, research, and solve problems independently.

This experience stayed with me throughout my career. Any time someone asks for my help, I try not just to give an answer, but to guide them through the thinking process. Because the goal is not just solving the immediate problem—it's developing people who can solve problems long after you're gone.

Learning to Step Back

Years later, when I had already grown into higher leadership roles, I received feedback that forced me to reflect on the other side of mentoring. A CFO once told me:

"Héctor, your leadership is too strong. Sometimes people on your team cannot be seen as leaders, because the operators, supervisors, and even the union members all come directly to you. They wait for you to return to solve problems or make decisions, and that takes away leadership presence from your managers on the floor."

At first, I didn't understand. How could my leadership take away from someone else's? I had worked side by side with operators, solved problems directly, and built trust with the teams. Naturally, people came to me. But after reflecting, I realized he was right. I had moved from being a day-to-day problem solver to a director overseeing multiple areas, yet I was still stepping into details and giving direct instructions.

I needed to change. Instead of being the visible fixer of problems, I had to become the mentor behind the curtain. When I walked to the floor and saw issues, I stopped giving immediate answers. Instead, I directed my observations to supervisors and managers, guiding them on how to analyze the situation, challenge assumptions, and come back to me with their own solutions. My role shifted from solving the problem myself to ensuring others were developing the ability to solve it.

I assured them: *"If you make a mistake, we'll solve it together. You have my support, because what I'm asking of you is to grow as a leader, not to be perfect."*

Over time, the results became clear. One day, I heard someone in an exit interview ask, *"Why do we even have a director? All the managers are the ones resolving the issues."* At first, that could have felt like an insult. But instead, I smiled inside. That comment meant my strategy was working. The managers were now the recognized leaders. The people on the floor no longer saw me as the problem solver—they saw their own managers as the ones to go to.

That was the whole intention. By stepping back, I allowed new leaders to step forward.

The Ripple Effect

One of the most rewarding things I've witnessed is the ripple effect of mentorship. When you invest in others, they naturally pass it on. I've seen technicians mentor apprentices, engineers mentor interns, and supervisors' mentor new hires—each person building on what was given to them. Leadership multiplies when a culture of mentoring takes root.

But the opposite is also true: if leaders hoard knowledge, organizations stagnate. Growth stops. A company becomes dependent on one or two people instead of being sustained by a strong team.

The Legacy of Mentorship

One of my proudest moments as a leader has not been tied to KPIs, profits, or even the successful turnaround of a facility. Those things matter, but they fade with time. What truly stayed with me is seeing the people I once worked with—and with whom I shared a little of my knowledge—rise to become Directors, COOs, and even owners of their own companies.

I stay in contact with many of them, and just as I share with others who inspired me, they often tell me what they remember from our time together. Some say, *"I'll never forget when you challenged me to solve a problem on my own."* Others recall, *"You told me not to be discouraged, but to take a mistake as an opportunity to grow—and to make sure it never happened again."* Still others tell me, *"You gave me confidence because I knew I couldn't fail. Even if I made a mistake, you would help me fix it. You always had my back."*

Those are the stories that matter. The fact that someone remembers a single phrase, a challenge, or a moment of encouragement years later is more meaningful to me than any production report. Because those memories shape careers, families, and futures far beyond the walls of a plant.

By the end of the day, the real question is not how many projects you delivered or how much profit you generated, but **what your legacy was when you left this world.** For me, that legacy lives in the people I was privileged to mentor. It lives in the leaders they became and the way they, in turn, will pass it forward.

That is one of the main reasons I share these stories through my books. If even one story makes someone smile, think differently, or push themselves to grow, then I know I've left something behind that matters.

The Balance of Challenge and Support

Great mentors do two things: they **challenge** and they **support**. Too much challenge without support discourages. Too much support without challenge creates comfort zones. The art of mentoring is knowing when to push someone beyond their limits and when to stand beside them to reassure them.

I often told my teams: *"I won't let you drown, but I will let you swim on your own."*

Challenge for the Reader

Think about your own leadership journey. Who mentored you? Who believed in you before you believed in yourself? More importantly, who are you mentoring right now?

- Identify **one person** in your team or circle that you can intentionally mentor.
- Don't wait for the perfect program or setting—start with a conversation.
- Share a lesson from your own story, ask them questions, and give them space to grow.

Your leadership legacy will not be written only in results—it will be written in people.

Chapter 24. The Leader's Horizon: Balancing Today and Tomorrow

"You can't protect tomorrow if you're always fighting today's fires."

In Chapter 16, we looked at how leaders must manage their personal energy to stay effective. But leadership is not only about sustaining yourself — it's also about sustaining the organization. This chapter shifts the focus to a broader horizon: delivering results today while building the future.

One of the greatest tensions in leadership is navigating the urgent needs of today while preparing for the realities of tomorrow. Most organizations live in a cycle of short-term pressures: monthly numbers, quarterly targets, year-end reviews. Yet the leaders who leave lasting legacies are those who look beyond the quarter — they see the horizon.

Short-Term Wins vs. Long-Term Vision

The truth is, both are necessary. Without short-term execution, the company doesn't survive. Without long-term planning, it doesn't evolve. The best leaders are those who build systems and cultures that deliver results today while preparing the ground for tomorrow.

I've seen too many organizations burn out by chasing immediate wins: pushing equipment past its limits, overloading top talent until they quit, or cutting training and safety investments to save money in the quarter. The books may look good today, but the cost always shows up tomorrow — in breakdowns, turnover, and lost trust.

By contrast, the companies that invest in people, technology, and future capabilities often look slower at first. But they are the ones that thrive five, ten, or twenty years later.

The Cost of Neglecting the Future

In one facility I joined, leadership bonuses were tied only to units shipped. To maximize short-term numbers, critical investments were postponed — training, safety upgrades, and even long-term contracts with suppliers. For a while, it looked like success. But within two years, the costs hit: higher accidents, missed deliveries, and breakdowns that shut down entire lines. The leaders had already moved on, but the team left behind paid the price.

That experience reinforced a simple truth: **you always pay for the future — the only question is whether you pay now in preparation or later in crisis.**

A Story of Long-Term Vision: The Green Bay Forging Facility

One of the clearest examples of balancing today with tomorrow came during the planning of our new Green Bay forging facility. On paper, the decision looked overwhelming: millions in capital investment, years before we would see the full return, and countless hurdles in design, permitting, and construction. It would have been easier — and cheaper — to push our existing equipment harder, patch problems as they came, and squeeze a few more years out of the old infrastructure.

But deep down, we all knew that would only delay the inevitable. Our customers were demanding forgings with **tighter specifications**, higher consistency, and competitive pricing in a global market where countries like India and China were pressing hard. The old machines could not deliver that future. If we waited until the equipment failed, we would be reacting in crisis mode. By planning years ahead, we had the chance to build something world-class with **state-of-the-art equipment**.

One of the strategies that made this vision possible was the way our leadership divided responsibilities. The **CEO and CFO focused on the future state** — securing funding and managing the financial foundation for the investment — while I focused on making sure, we could support those plans with **efficient day-to-day operations and customer alignment**. It was a partnership of horizons: one eye on tomorrow, one eye on today.

Walking through that facility as it came together reminded me what leadership vision truly means. You aren't just solving today's problems; you are laying down a path others will walk for decades.

The payoff wasn't immediate — it never is. But the moment we struck our first billets in Green Bay, I knew the sacrifices and sleepless nights had been worth it. We had built not just capacity, but confidence — in our people, our process, and our future.

Tools for Balancing Today and Tomorrow

Leaders can avoid the trap of short-term thinking by using a few key practices:

- **Set Dual Metrics**: Measure success not only by today's output, but by tomorrow's readiness, training hours completed, preventive actions taken, employee development, innovation projects.
- **Create Rolling Plans**: Think in three horizons — today's quarter, the next 12 months, and the next 3–5 years. Keep all three visible.
- **Protect Time for Strategy**: Block moments in the calendar not for operations, but for vision. A leader who never looks up from the floor can't see the horizon.
- **Invest in People**: Skills, careers, and leadership pipelines don't appear overnight. Long-term results are built on long-term development.

- **Tell the Story of the Future**: Teams execute better when they understand not only the "what" but the "why." Explain how today's discipline is building tomorrow's success.

Frameworks for Long-Term Leadership

While personal discipline is essential, there are also powerful frameworks that help leaders balance today and tomorrow.

1. EOS (Entrepreneurial Operating System)

Popularized by Gino Wickman in *Traction*, EOS helps leaders create clarity and execution by breaking down the horizon into manageable chunks.

- **Vision**: Aligning everyone on where the organization is going.
- **Traction**: Converting vision into 90-day "rocks" (short-term, measurable goals).
- **People & Process**: Ensuring the right people are in the right roles and following clear, repeatable systems.

EOS reminds us that vision without execution is just a dream, and execution without vision is just activity. Leaders must unite both.

2. Hoshin Kanri (Policy Deployment)

Used widely in Lean organizations, Hoshin Kanri connects long-term breakthrough objectives (3–5 years) with annual goals, team-level targets, and daily actions.

- Strategy is "cascaded down" through every level.
- Progress is checked regularly in a "catchball" process, where feedback flows both ways.

It ensures that every operator, supervisor, and executive knows how their work today contributes to tomorrow's success.

3. Balanced Scorecard

Developed by Kaplan and Norton, the Balanced Scorecard encourages leaders to measure success from four perspectives:

- **Financial**: Are we profitable today?
- **Customer**: Are we delivering real value?
- **Internal Processes**: Are we efficient, reliable, and innovative?
- **Learning & Growth**: Are we developing people and capabilities for the future?

This framework prevents leaders from focusing only on immediate financial performance while neglecting the investments that sustain long-term strength.

4. Three Horizons Model

This model helps leaders distribute energy and resources wisely:

- **Horizon 1**: Strengthening the core business (today).
- **Horizon 2**: Developing adjacent opportunities (next 2–3 years).
- **Horizon 3**: Exploring disruptive innovations for the future.

It reminds us that leaders must both protect the present and prepare for what's next.

Closing Reflection

Leadership is not only about what you deliver this quarter, but about what you leave behind. A good leader balances urgency with vision, execution with foresight, today with tomorrow.

The horizon is always out there — and while you may never fully reach it, your ability to keep your eyes on it while guiding your team forward defines the kind of legacy you will leave.

Reader Reflection

A leader's greatest responsibility is not only to deliver results today, but to ensure the organization is stronger tomorrow. Short-term victories are satisfying, but they fade. Long-term planning, though less visible in the moment, creates the foundation others will build upon.

Ask yourself:

- Am I spending most of my energy solving today's problems, or preparing for tomorrow's opportunities?
- Do my team's metrics measure only output, or also readiness for the future?
- If I left my role tomorrow, would I leave behind systems, people, and processes strong enough to thrive without me?

Challenge

This week, review your calendar, goals, or metrics.

- Identify **one area** where you are focused purely on short-term results.
- Redesign it to also support long-term success — whether that means scheduling preventive actions, planning training, or setting a vision beyond the next quarter.

Share the "why" with your team. Show them how today's discipline creates tomorrow's strength.

That's how leaders not only meet the moment but shape the future.

Unlike Chapter 16, which focused on a leader's personal energy, this chapter has been about protecting the organization's long-term health. In the next chapter, we will shift the lens once more — this time to life outside the workplace. Because just as leaders must plan for their companies' futures, they must also guard the family, relationships, and well-being that give their work meaning.

Chapter 25. Resilience and Well-Being: Balancing Leadership and Life

"Resilience is built in recovery, not endurance."

Earlier, in Chapter 16, we explored how leaders must care for their own energy, and in Chapter 24, how they must protect the organization's future. This chapter is different: it is about the personal side of leadership — protecting yourself and your family from the cost of neglect and remembering why you chose this path in the first place.

Leadership is often described as a marathon, not a sprint. Yet too many leaders approach it like a series of exhausting sprints — rushing from crisis to crisis, pushing themselves to their limits, and believing that sacrifice is the only way to succeed. What I have learned through decades in demanding industries is that no matter how skilled, visionary, or determined a leader may be, leadership without resilience is unsustainable.

The Cost of Neglecting Well-Being

There will always be regrets in life. At different moments, I have asked myself: *Could I have done things differently? Could I have done them better?* My goal was simple but powerful — to be a provider. I wanted to make sure my family never had to worry about a hot meal, a warm bed, a safe roof over our heads, a reliable means of transportation, and opportunities to enjoy life together — trips, movies, family moments.

For me, striving for a higher salary or a higher position was never about competing with others or even with myself. It was always about ensuring that I could provide these things for my family. Instead of wishing for lottery winnings or seeking shortcuts that might compromise my values, I chose to work hard, ethically, and honestly. Every step, every promotion, every accomplishment was earned. I could look in the mirror and say, *"I worked for this. I earned it."* That pride carried me through the long hours, the stress, and the sacrifices.

But how much is too much? There were stretches when days would go by without my family really seeing me. I justified it by telling myself that I was solving problems that protected the organization, and that I loved the challenge. The more I told myself this, the easier it became to rationalize my absence.

And yet, the regrets remain. I missed some of my daughter's recitals. I told myself the videotapes would make up for it, but they didn't. The impact of not being there in person left a mark. Looking back, I believe I tried, but responsibility often kept me in the office longer than I should have stayed.

Building Personal Resilience

Resilience doesn't mean being unshakable; it means being able to bend without breaking. Leaders face setbacks, criticism, and pressure every day. Developing resilience requires habits and mindsets that allow recovery:

- **Perspective.** Challenges are temporary, and even failures can become lessons that shape future success.
- **Health.** Sleep, exercise, and proper nutrition aren't luxuries. They are leadership tools as critical as strategy meetings or financial reports.
- **Boundaries.** Knowing when to disconnect from work — to rest, to recharge, to be present with family — ensures you return stronger.
- **Reflection.** Taking time to review not only what went wrong but also what went right keeps hope and motivation alive.

The Role of Relationships

No leader thrives alone. Spouses, children, friends, mentors, and even colleagues form the support systems that carry leaders through difficult seasons. In my own journey, moments of exhaustion were balanced by the encouragement of my wife and daughter, by mentors who reminded me of the bigger picture, and by teams that lifted one another.

The paradox of leadership is that while leaders often feel alone at the top, they are never truly alone if they are willing to let others in. Sharing burdens, asking for help, and investing in relationships is not a weakness — it is a source of strength.

Modeling Balance for Others

When leaders embrace resilience and well-being, they set an example for their teams. A culture that values rest, respect, and healthy limits is far more sustainable than one built on fear and exhaustion. As leaders, we do not only manage projects; we model what success should look like. If we normalize burnout, our teams will mirror it. If we normalize balance, they will mirror that too.

That is why I believe this chapter is not just advice — it is a message for every future manager, director, and COO: work family time and personal time into your agenda. Treat it like any other task on your calendar. Because that task — taking care of the reason you started this journey in the first place — is the most important one of all.

Lessons Learned

1. **Resilience is a choice, not a gift.** It comes from daily practices that protect your mind, body, and spirit.
2. **Well-being is strategic.** A leader's health directly impacts organizational health.
3. **Balance is dynamic.** There will always be seasons of intensity, but they must be followed by seasons of recovery.
4. **Your legacy is measured at home as much as in the workplace.** Titles and results fade, but relationships endure.

Reader Reflection

- How often do you check in on your own energy, health, and emotional state?
- What boundaries do you need to set to protect your well-being?
- Who are the people you lean on, and how can you strengthen those connections?
- What example are you setting for your team when it comes to balance and resilience?

Challenge

This week, identify one practice you can adopt to strengthen your resilience — whether it's setting aside time for exercise, committing to a digital-free evening with family, or journaling at the end of each day. Protect that practice fiercely. Over time, these habits become the foundation that allows you not only to lead but to endure and to thrive.

Suggested Reading

For readers who want to explore these ideas more deeply, here are a few excellent books:

- **"Resilient: How to Grow an Unshakable Core of Calm, Strength, and Happiness"** by Rick Hanson
- **"The Power of Full Engagement"** by Jim Loehr and Tony Schwartz
- **"Daring Greatly"** by Brené Brown
- **"The Burnout Epidemic"** by Jennifer Moss
- **"Leaders Eat Last"** by Simon Sinek

Closing Note

As I look back, I realize that leadership is not only about what you build, fix, or grow in the workplace — it is also about what you protect and nurture at home. Resilience and balance ensure that the leader does not lose sight of the very reasons they began this journey in the first place.

And so, as we move into the final words of this book, I want to leave you not just with lessons from factories and boardrooms, but with a personal reminder: leadership is both professional and profoundly human. It is not about perfection, but about presence.

If Chapter 16 reminded you to keep your own tank full, and Chapter 24 challenged you to look at the organization's horizon, this chapter is about remembering the people at home who are part of your journey. Because leadership is not only professional — it is profoundly personal.

Chapter 26. Leading in Crisis: Calm in the Storm

"In crisis, people follow your calm long before they follow your plan."

During my career I have faced many stressful situations, moments when everything seemed to fall apart at once. Over the years, people have told me, *"You always look so calm during a crisis."*
The truth is, I wasn't calm inside. My stomach was tight, my mind was racing, and I'm sure I developed a few ulcers along the way.

But as a leader, panic is a luxury you cannot afford. Your calmness becomes the anchor others hold onto. When everything around you is chaos, you must remain centered enough to think clearly—to protect your people first, secure the equipment second, and safeguard the operation as a whole.

The First Pour

One Sunday night, at the start of a new foundry's very first shift, I learned this lesson once again. We used to say:

If the night shift runs well, the week will run well. But if the first shift starts badly, expect a rough week.

I had traveled from Saltillo to Monterrey to oversee the startup. Everything looked perfect—the molding line was running, the furnaces had melted the first batches, the chemistry was within spec, the core setup machines were ready, and every operator was present.

Relieved, I called my wife: "Everything's running smoothly. I'll be home soon."
I shut off my computer, turned off the lights, and opened the door—only to be greeted by a sight no foundry manager wants to see.

The Floor of Fire

The floor was glowing orange. Molten metal—2,500 pounds of it—covered the ground, hissing and cracking the concrete beneath. The heat was intense, panic spread quickly among the crew.

I shouted, "Don't run! Stay calm. Stay away from the area." Then I called for the forklift operator to bring barrels of green sand from outside and told the rest of the team to grab shovels.

When the sand arrived, I instructed them to pour it over the molten metal to contain it and begin cooling it down.
Within minutes, everyone was working together. The orange glow faded to dull red, then gray, then solid. We had contained the problem. No one was hurt.

Understanding What Happened

Once it was safe, we began the cleanup and called a meeting to find out what went wrong. I phoned my wife again: "I spoke too soon. I'll be here all night."

Our investigation revealed the cause. The ladle operator, using a remote control, lifted too early, catching the ladle on the furnace cover. Instead of lowering it, he panicked and pulled harder flipping the entire ladle and spilling the molten steel onto the floor.

Engineering a Permanent Solution

That night we committed to ensuring this would never happen again. Together with our maintenance and engineering teams, we designed a new safety interlock system. Once the ladle passed a certain point, it could not be lifted until sensors confirmed it was safe.

While the engineering solution was being built, we marked the floor with clear safety zones, trained every shift, and reviewed procedures. The improvement worked flawlessly. The lesson was clear: every crisis must produce a better system, not just a quick fix.

Calm Is Contagious

That night reinforced a truth I've carried through every leadership challenge:

When you stay calm, others stay capable.

Fear is natural. But composure allows reason to lead emotion. Inside, I was anxious and exhausted; outside, I needed to be steady and decisive. That composure kept people safe and allowed the team to transform a near-disaster into a learning experience that made the foundry stronger.

Guidelines for Leading in Times of Crisis

Crises will come—fires, breakdowns, financial shocks, or unexpected personnel issues. What defines a leader is not the absence of fear, but the ability to guide others through it. Here are some lessons that have helped me lead when everything seemed to be falling apart:

1. **Protect People First.**
   Nothing matters more than safety. Make sure everyone is accounted for, injuries are prevented, and emergency procedures are followed. Equipment can be replaced lives cannot.
2. **Stay Physically and Verbally Calm.**
   Your tone, posture, and words set the emotional temperature of the room. A calm leader gives confidence even when the outcome is uncertain.

3. **Slow Down to Think Clearly.**
   In chaos, speed can kill. Take a breath before deciding. A few seconds of clarity are worth more than ten minutes of panic.
4. **Communicate Openly and Often.**
   Silence fuels fear. Even if you don't have all the answers, share what you know. Transparency builds trust, and trust stabilizes teams.
5. **Assign Roles and Empower Quickly.**
   People want to help in a crisis. Give them direction—specific, actionable steps. Clear delegation prevents confusion and shows confidence in your team.
6. **Document and Debrief.**
   Once the immediate danger is over, investigate thoroughly. Understand what failed, why, and how to prevent it. Crises are expensive teachers; make the tuition worth it.
7. **Implement Permanent Corrective Actions.**
   Don't settle for temporary fixes. Engineer long-term solutions, train everyone, and follow up to ensure they stay in place.
8. **Take Care of Yourself.**
   After the crisis, decompress. Stress hides quietly until it catches up with you. Rest, reflect, and learn—your future calm will depend on it.

Manager's Exercise: Simulating Calm Under Pressure

Objective:
To practice decision-making, communication, and emotional control during a simulated crisis.

Instructions:

1. **Create a scenario.**
   Gather your team and describe a realistic workplace cri-

sis—such as a machine breakdown, quality issue, supply shortage, or safety incident.
2. **Assign roles.**
Choose team members to play specific roles: operator, maintenance lead, quality inspector, HR, or customer service representative.
3. **Set the timer for 10 minutes.**
During that time, act as the leader in charge. Respond to the situation as if it were real—asking questions, making decisions, and directing actions.
4. **Observe your behavior.**
Pay attention to your tone of voice, posture, and clarity of instruction. Did you stay calm? Did you empower others or take over everything yourself?
5. **Debrief together.**
After the exercise, discuss what went well and what could improve. Encourage honest feedback from your team.

Reflection Questions:

- How did your body react when pressure increased?
- Did your communication help calm or escalate the situation?
- What steps will you take to prepare for real crises in the future?

Key Lesson:

Calm leadership can be trained. By practicing it in controlled environments, you condition your mind to respond with clarity instead of panic when real crises strike.

Final Reflection

Leadership in crisis is about balance—between emotion and logic, fear and focus, urgency and patience.

Every storm eventually passes, but the way you behave during it becomes part of your legacy.

As leaders, we are not judged only by how we perform when things go right, but by how we respond when everything goes wrong. The calm you project becomes the bridge between chaos and recovery.

That is what it means to lead in crisis—to be the calm in the storm.

Every crisis reveals something deeper about leadership, it strips away the noise and exposes what truly matters: people, trust, and adaptability.

As organizations expand across borders and cultures, the ability to remain calm under pressure must evolve into the ability to lead with understanding across differences. The next chapter explores how global and diverse teams challenge us to broaden our definition of leadership—one that values not only composure, but also empathy, inclusion, and perspective.

The calm you project becomes not just the bridge between chaos and recovery, but between people and cultures

Chapter 27. Diversity and Global Leadership
"A global leader listens to understand—not to confirm."

Leading Beyond Borders and Differences

A Lesson from the Plant Floor

I still remember a project that brought together engineers from Germany, operators from Mexico, and supervisors from the United States. Everyone had a different way of working, a different rhythm, even a different sense of humor.
At first, what was supposed to be collaboration felt more like controlled chaos. The German team wanted everything documented in detail before taking any action. The Mexican crew wanted to adapt on the fly, and the Americans tried to find balance between the two. Meetings were filled with tension, and misunderstandings piled up quickly.

But then something changed. We stopped debating who was right and started asking why each team approached the work that way. The Germans were driven by structure, the Mexicans by creativity, and the Americans by practicality. Once we recognized those strengths instead of fighting them, the project took off. Production improved, and relationships followed.

That experience taught me one of the most powerful lessons in leadership:
diversity is not about managing differences—it's about unlocking potential through understanding.

Understanding the Power of Diversity

Diversity goes beyond nationality or language. It includes gender, age, experience, and the unique way each person sees the world. A leader who values diversity doesn't just count how many different people are in the room—he makes sure each one is heard.

When everyone feels safe to contribute ideas, innovation becomes natural. A young engineer challenging an old method, a technician suggesting a new layout, or a manager proposing a cultural exchange—these moments spark progress. Homogeneous teams can execute; diverse teams can transform.

The leader's responsibility is to create the environment where those ideas can breathe. That means listening without judgment and leading without ego.

Cultural Intelligence: The New Leadership Skill

Technical knowledge used to be the most valued skill in manufacturing. Today, cultural intelligence, the ability to connect across backgrounds—is equally important.
Leaders who can read unspoken cues, respect traditions, and adapt their communication style are the ones who build trust across borders.

When I first worked with international teams, I learned that communication isn't only about what we say, it's also about what we mean. A "yes" can mean agreement in one culture, but politeness in another. A pause can mean reflection—or resistance. Learning to read those signals takes time and humility, but once you master it, you lead with empathy instead of authority.

Cultural intelligence is not about changing who you are, it's about expanding your awareness so you can meet people where they are.

Global Leadership Is Personal

Being a global leader doesn't require a passport requires perspective.
You don't have to cross an ocean to lead diverse people; diversity

exists in every community and organization. True global leadership starts with curiosity and grows through respect.

Over the years, I've learned that people everywhere share the same desires: to be respected, trusted, and given a purpose. Whether in a small plant in Monterrey or a large facility in Michigan, human values are universal.
The tools, systems, and languages may differ, but the need for recognition and dignity remains the same.

Leading globally is not about managing others—it's about connecting with humanity.

Key Takeaways

Diversity is strength. It multiplies perspectives, creativity, and problem-solving.
Cultural intelligence matters. Understanding others' values builds bridges faster than authority ever will.
Inclusion requires action. It's not enough to invite people to the table; leaders must make room for their voices.
Global leadership begins locally. Every interaction is a chance to learn from someone's world.
Empathy is the universal language. It transcends borders, titles, and time zones.

Challenge for the Reader

Over the next few weeks, challenge yourself to **lead with curiosity and inclusion**—not just across countries, but across perspectives.

1. **Seek one conversation** with someone whose background, culture, or approach to work differs from your own. Ask about

their experiences, what motivates them, and how they see leadership. Listen without trying to correct or compare—just understand.
2. **Invite a new voice to the table.** In your next meeting or project discussion, ask for input from someone who doesn't usually speak up. Show genuine interest and highlight their contribution.
3. **Reflect on your own biases.** Write down two assumptions you often make about people based on where they're from, their experience, or how they communicate. Then, challenge those assumptions by seeking real examples that prove them wrong.
4. **Celebrate one act of cross-cultural collaboration.** Share a success story—big or small—where different perspectives led to a better result. Use it as a teaching moment for your team.

Global leadership begins in the way we treat those closest to us. When you intentionally listen, include, and learn from people different than yourself, you expand not only your leadership—but your humanity.

Final Reflection:

The world no longer rewards leaders who demand conformity—it celebrates those who inspire collaboration.
As dreamers who lead, our goal is not to erase differences but to unite them toward a common vision. Because when we learn to lead beyond borders, we stop seeing a map—and start seeing people.

Chapter 28. Sustainability and Responsibility in Leadership
"A leader's duty is to deliver progress without debt to the future."

Leadership is not only about achieving results; it's about ensuring that the way we reach them leaves the world better than we found it. True leaders understand that every decision—no matter how technical or operational—has ripple effects that touch people, communities, and the environment. Sustainability is not just a corporate goal; it's a reflection of responsibility, foresight, and integrity.

I've learned over the years that sustainability begins with awareness. In manufacturing, it's easy to focus on production numbers, throughput, and cost reduction, but sustainability challenges us to ask a deeper question: *At what cost?* Are we consuming more than we can replace? Are we prioritizing short-term gains over long-term stability? These are not only environmental questions, they are leadership questions.

In one of my plants, I remember facing a situation where equipment upgrades were needed. The cheaper option involved retrofitting older, less efficient systems that consumed more energy and required more frequent maintenance. The alternative was a significant investment in new energy-efficient machinery that would reduce waste, lower emissions, and create a safer working environment. Initially, the finance team resisted. The payback seemed long, and the benefits weren't immediately visible on a quarterly report. But as leaders, we must see beyond the next quarter; we must look toward the next decade.

We chose the sustainable option. It wasn't the easiest path, but over time, the benefits were undeniable, reduced costs, higher reliability, and a proud workforce that knew their efforts were contributing to something larger than production metrics. That's the kind of responsibility that multiplies its own value.

Sustainability is not only environmental; it's also **social**. It involves the way we treat our people, our communities, and our reputation. A leader who neglects the human side of sustainability eventually pays the price in morale, turnover, and lost trust. Responsibility means making decisions that protect not only the company's future but also the dignity and well-being of those who make that future possible.

Transparency plays a major role here. Whether it's admitting mistakes, owning up to an operational misstep, or confronting the ethical implications of a business decision, responsible leadership requires courage. Many leaders avoid uncomfortable conversations in the name of efficiency—but responsibility means confronting what's uncomfortable before it becomes unmanageable.

Another form of sustainability is **personal**. Leaders must take care of themselves to serve others effectively. Burning out, neglecting health, or losing balance in pursuit of goals doesn't just affect the individual, it weakens the entire organization. Sustainable leadership means managing energy, not just time. It's about leading with consistency, clarity, and authenticity over the long run.

How Leadership Can Support Sustainability

To move from intention to action, leaders can integrate sustainability into daily operations and long-term strategy by:

1. **Embedding sustainability into the company's vision and KPIs** – Treat environmental and social metrics with the same importance as financial results.
2. **Championing innovation and efficiency** – Encourage cross-functional teams to find creative ways to reduce waste, energy use, and costs through lean manufacturing, automation, and smart design.

3. **Educating and engaging employees** – Sustainability thrives when everyone understands its purpose. Provide training, recognize ideas, and make employees part of the process.
4. **Partnering with suppliers and customers** – Choose partners who share similar values. Work together to create transparent supply chains and shared sustainability goals.
5. **Measuring impact and communicating progress** – Publish sustainability reports or internal updates to celebrate milestones and maintain accountability.
6. **Supporting community programs** – Contribute to education, environmental restoration, and local development initiatives that strengthen the communities around your organization.
7. **Fostering diversity and inclusion** – Encourage different perspectives and ideas; innovation flourishes when everyone has a voice.
8. **Setting an example through ethical leadership** – Make decisions that demonstrate integrity, even when no one is watching.

Resources and Networks for Sustainable Leadership

Leaders can draw inspiration, support, and knowledge from a variety of sources:

- **United Nations Sustainable Development Goals (UN SDGs)** – A global framework for guiding sustainability initiatives.
- **Environmental Protection Agency (EPA)** – For compliance, efficiency standards, and energy-saving programs.
- **ISO 14001 Certification** – For implementing and maintaining environmental management systems.
- **Global Reporting Initiative (GRI)** – For standardized sustainability reporting and transparency.

- **Local Chambers of Commerce and Industry Associations** – For community-driven programs and sustainability partnerships.
- **Educational institutions and leadership programs** – Many universities and organizations now offer executive courses focused on sustainable management and ESG (Environmental, Social, and Governance) principles.

Reader Reflection

Take a moment to reflect on how sustainability and responsibility appear in your own leadership.
Are your daily decisions focused only on short-term goals—or do they also consider long-term impact?
Think about your plant, office, or team. Where are you wasting resources—time, energy, or even human potential?
Sustainability begins with awareness, but it grows through action. Each of us influences how responsibly our organizations operate—whether by reducing material waste, improving safety, strengthening community ties, or developing people for the future.

True sustainability isn't just about protecting the planet—it's about protecting purpose.
When leaders align business results with ethical responsibility, they build companies that last and legacies that matter.

Challenge for the Reader

In the next 30 days, take intentional steps to integrate sustainability and responsibility into your leadership decisions:

1. Identify one area of waste in your operation—energy, materials, or time—and develop a plan to reduce or eliminate it.

2. Engage your team. Ask for one idea from every department or crew on how they can contribute to sustainability or social responsibility. Recognize and implement the most practical ideas.
3. Partner with purpose. Reach out to a local organization, school, or community initiative where your team can make a tangible difference—through education, mentoring, or environmental support.
4. Model personal sustainability. Commit to one habit that helps you sustain yourself as a leader—rest, exercise, mindfulness, or family time. Remember, responsible leadership begins with self-care.
5. Measure and share progress. At the end of the month, share results with your team. Celebrate small wins, discuss what didn't work, and set a new sustainability goal for the next quarter.

Leadership that values sustainability builds more than profit—it builds trust, pride, and a legacy that endures.
Every decision is a chance to choose between short-term success and long-term significance. Choose wisely.

Leadership Reflection

In the end, sustainability and responsibility are not external goals, they are reflections of who we are as leaders. The world doesn't need more managers who deliver results at any cost; it needs more leaders who deliver progress with purpose.

Sustainability is not about perfection; it's about direction. Every action, every policy, and every decision can either add to the problem or become part of the solution. True leadership is measured not just by what we build, but by what we preserve.

Our legacy as leaders will not be defined by the machines we installed, the products we made, or the profits we achieved, it will be defined by the impact we left on people, the environment, and the generations that follow.

Chapter 29. Final Words from a Dreamer Who Leads
"Every leader is shaped by their story—yours is still being written."

Every journey eventually reaches a point where the road bends into the unknown—where reflection meets anticipation. **For me, that bend represents not an end, but a new beginning.** *Dreamers Who Lead* has been a collection of lessons, failures, victories, and realizations shaped by decades of leadership, transformation, and human connection. Yet, this chapter is not an ending—it is a continuation of the path that began long ago with a simple idea: that leadership is not a title, but a responsibility to others and to oneself.

The Essence of Leadership

Leadership, at its core, is not about control; it is about influence. It's the art of guiding others toward a shared purpose while never losing sight of your own integrity. True leaders inspire through consistency—by showing up even when no one else does, by being transparent when mistakes happen, and by believing in people long before they believe in themselves.

Great leaders are not born; they are forged—through pressure, doubt, and perseverance. They understand that success is not the absence of failure but the mastery of learning from it. They carry scars, not as reminders of pain, but as proof of growth.

The Reality of Leadership

Being a leader is not always easy. There will be personal sacrifices, moments of solitude, and decisions that weigh heavily. There will be critics—people who are quick to point out mistakes but rarely offer solutions or take action themselves. When that happens, don't feel discouraged. Because in the end, people remember those who dared to try, who dared to dream, and more importantly, who dared to implement.

A true leader walks into the unknown to build a path that is safe for others to follow—one that future teams will not only walk but also improve upon. Nothing meaningful can be accomplished alone. Building trust takes time, but it begins with small, consistent successes. Once people see results, they start to believe. They follow because they see the vision come to life. Everyone wants to be part of success—but not everyone is willing to work hard to achieve it. A leader's role is to ignite that belief and to keep the flame alive even when others doubt.

The Legacy of a Dreamer

To dream is to believe in what doesn't yet exist. To lead is to make that dream possible for others. The two are inseparable. Every dreamer who becomes a leader takes on the responsibility of turning imagination into motion.

As I look back at my own road—from the small border town where I was born to boardrooms and forging plants across continents, I realize that leadership is not measured by titles, machines, or metrics. It's measured by the lives you've touched, the trust you've earned, and the courage you've shown when the outcome was uncertain.

A Call to the Next Generation

To those who read these words and feel the same fire—the desire to build, improve, and inspire—remember this:
You do not need permission to lead. You only need conviction. Leadership starts with small actions—listening before judging, caring before commanding, and learning before deciding.

Surround yourself with people who challenge you to grow, not just those who make you comfortable. Be humble enough to ask questions, and brave enough to act when no one else will. The world does not need more bosses—it needs more dreamers who lead.

Closing Reflection

The road of leadership is endless. Every project, every decision, every team is another chapter in a story that outlives us. And just like *The Road of a Dreamer*, this book represents not a conclusion, but a handoff—a torch passed to those who believe that purpose and leadership can coexist.

As you walk your own path, may you remember:
Leadership is not about being the best.
It's about making others better because you were there.
And at the end of every challenge, every success, every long day… may you look back and smile, knowing that you led not out of fear or ego, but out of love for what could be.

Because that is the true mark of a dreamer who leads.

Epilogue: The Road Continues

When I wrote *The Road of a Dreamer*, it was an act of remembrance — a journey back through the places, faces, and choices that shaped who I became. It was about identity, resilience, and the courage to believe when the path ahead was unclear. It was a story of one dreamer learning to walk.

Dreamers Who Lead is the next step — the moment when that same dreamer realizes that walking alone is never enough. To lead means to create a road that others can follow, to use the lessons earned through struggle to make someone else's path a little smoother, a little safer, a little clearer.

If *The Road of a Dreamer* was about finding purpose, this book is about sharing it. It is the natural continuation of a promise — that our dreams don't end when we reach them; they evolve when we help others reach theirs.

Through the years, I've learned that leadership is not a destination. It's a living journey, one that requires humility, persistence, and heart. Every new challenge brings another opportunity to teach, to listen, to grow. And every person you encounter becomes part of your legacy — a reflection of what you stood for when it mattered most.

To every dreamer reading this: Keep walking. Keep believing. And when you've gone far enough to see the view from the top, remember to look back — and build a bridge for those still climbing.

Because the road never ends… it simply changes travelers.
And that is how dreamers become leaders.

Acknowledgments

This book was not written in isolation, reflects years of lessons, challenges, and the many people who walked beside me.

To colleagues, mentors, and teammates across foundries, forges, and factories: thank you for teaching me lessons no textbook ever could. Through your work, your silence, and your example, you shaped my understanding of leadership.

To the executives, managers, and engineers I've partnered with, thank you for the trust and opportunities that allowed me to lead, fail, learn, and grow.

To my creative collaborators, especially ChatGPT by OpenAI, thank you for helping me organize and refine these stories into a book that I hope will guide others on their leadership journey.

To my family—Patricia and Anna—your love, patience, and encouragement are the foundation behind every page. To my brothers, to my mother and to the memory of my father, your example remains my compass.

Finally, to every reader who encouraged me after *The Road of a Dreamer*: this book exists because of you. Whether you followed me from that first journey or are joining me here for the first time, thank you. Your encouragement convinced me that sharing not only the dream, but also the lessons of leadership, could make a difference.

This book is for all of you.

About the Author

Héctor A. Ibarra is a global manufacturing and operations leader with decades of experience transforming organizations across North America and beyond.

Born in Piedras Negras, Coahuila, Mexico, Héctor's career has taken him from the production floor to executive leadership roles, guiding teams through complex challenges in the forging and casting industries.

He is the author of *The Road of a Dreamer* and *Dreamers Who Lead*, books that explore the human side of leadership—bridging personal growth, professional discipline, and the courage to dream.

Héctor currently serves as Chief Operating Officer of **W.E. Hoban Company**, leading strategic operations and new manufacturing initiatives, while continuing to mentor the next generation of leaders.

When not at work, he enjoys time with his wife Patricia and daughter Anna, creating new ideas under his brand **The Road of a Dreamer LLC**, which celebrates storytelling, leadership, and legacy building.

Follow his journey and learn more at **www.theroadofadreamer.com**

Also, by Héctor A. Ibarra

The Road of a Dreamer

An inspiring memoir that traces Héctor's journey from a small border town in Mexico to a life of global leadership. Filled with stories of perseverance, identity, and family, it's a reflection on what it means to dream—and the courage it takes to make those dreams real.

El Camino de un Soñador

The Spanish edition of *The Road of a Dreamer*—faithfully translated to preserve the original tone and emotion of the English version. A celebration of culture, family, and purpose for readers who believe that every dream begins with a single step.

Available Worldwode in Amazon.com, www.theroadofadreamer.com and many bookstores

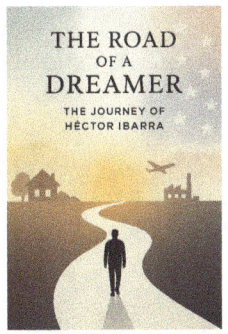
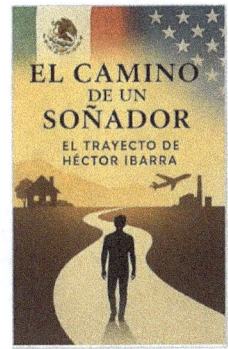

www.ingramcontent.com/pod-product-compliance
Lightning Source LLC
LaVergne TN
LVHW020427070526
838199LV00004B/306